MANIFEST IT NOW

Raise Your Vibration & Attract the Life You Desire – A Guide to Manifesting Wealth, Love, Success & Abundance

MONIKA DANIEL

© Copyright 2025 - All rights reserved. The contents of this book may not be reproduced, duplicated or transmitted without direct written permission from the author. Under no circumstances will any legal responsibility or blame be held against the publisher for any reparation, damages, or monetary loss due to the information herein, either directly or indirectly.

Legal Notice: This book is copyright protected. This is only for personal use. You cannot amend, distribute, sell, use, quote or paraphrase any part or the content within this book without the consent of the author.

Disclaimer Notice: Please note the information contained within this document is for educational and entertainment purposes only. Every attempt has been made to provide accurate, up to date and reliable complete information. No warranties of any kind are expressed or implied. Readers acknowledge that the author is not engaging in the rendering of legal, financial, medical or professional advice. The content of this book has been derived from various sources. Please consult a licensed professional before attempting any techniques outlined in this book. By reading this document, the reader agrees that under no circumstances is the author responsible for any losses, direct or indirect, which are incurred as a result of the use of information contained within this document, including, but not limited to, errors, omissions, or inaccuracies.

Contents

Why I Wrote This Book 1

Introduction 3

Chapter 1: The Manifestation Mindset 5

Chapter 2: Clarity is Power 21

Chapter 3: Energy and Emotion: The Frequency Factor 39

Chapter 4: The Law of Attraction Explained
(Without the Fluff) 57

Chapter 5: Speak It Into Existence – The Power of
Incantations 73

Chapter 6: Visualization, Affirmations, and Scripting 83

Chapter 7: Inspired Action vs. Forced Hustle 95

Chapter 8: Manifesting Money and Financial Freedom ... 109

Chapter 9: Love, Relationships & Soulmates 125

Chapter 10: When It's Not Working: Troubleshooting
Your Manifestation 139

Chapter 10: Your Manifestation Daily Routine 151

Conclusion: You Are the Creator of Your Reality 167

Bonus: Incantation Creation Worksheet 169

References 173

Why I Wrote This Book

For as long as I can remember, I've been fascinated by the idea that we have the power to shape our own lives. Over the years, I've discovered that the key to this is energy—how we can shift our thoughts, emotions, and actions to create the life we want.

My journey began years ago on the island of Koh Phangan in Thailand, where I first started learning about energy work and Reiki. What I quickly realized was that the same principles I used to heal my own energy could also help me attract the things I wanted—whether that was more peace, more success, or even more love.

I've seen it in my own life and in the lives of so many others: when you align your energy with what you truly desire, things start to fall into place. That's the magic of manifestation. It's not about wishing for things to happen—it's about learning how to tune into your own power and take aligned steps toward your goals.

This book is my way of sharing what I've learned. Whether you're new to manifestation or you've tried it before and things didn't work out, I want to show you how you can tap into your own ability to create change. Together, we'll explore practical ways to shift your mindset, get clear on your goals, and start attracting the life you've always wanted.

If you're ready to begin, I'm excited to guide you on this journey. Your dreams are waiting for you.

Introduction

Welcome to a new chapter in your life.

If you're holding this book, you're probably wondering how manifestation really works—and whether it's possible for you to use it to create the life you want. Maybe you've heard people talk about the Law of Attraction, or perhaps you've tried manifesting in the past and didn't see the results you were hoping for. Wherever you are on your journey, I'm here to tell you that manifestation is not only possible, but it's also within your reach right now.

This book is not just about thinking positively or hoping for the best. It's about understanding how your energy, thoughts, and emotions shape your reality—and learning how to use that power to your advantage. It's about discovering that you already have the tools within you to start creating change in your life. You're not waiting for something outside of yourself to shift. You're learning how to tap into your own potential.

You might be asking, "But how can I make this work for me?" That's exactly what we're going to explore together. I'll walk you through the steps, share personal stories of my own journey, and guide you with practical exercises that will help you shift your mindset, clear out any blocks, and open the door to what you truly want.

I've been where you are, unsure whether manifestation is just a wishful idea or if it's something real. Through my own experiences with Reiki and energy work, I've learned that the more we align ourselves with our desires—and the more we believe in our ability to receive them—the more they begin to show up in our lives. It's not magic. It's energy. And once you understand how to work with it, you'll be amazed at what's possible.

So let's get started. You have the power to create the life you want, and I'm here to show you how. I'm excited to be a part of your manifestation journey.

Chapter 1

The Manifestation Mindset

The Subconscious and How It Shapes Your Reality

The concept of manifestation may sound mystical, but at its core, it's based on one powerful principle: your thoughts and beliefs shape your reality. However, it's not just the thoughts you consciously think about during your day that are creating your life—it's the deeper, hidden thoughts in your subconscious mind that often have the most influence.

Think of your subconscious mind as the control center of your life. It's like the software running in the background of your computer—quiet, unnoticed, but constantly at work. Just as a computer can only operate based on the programs running inside it, your life unfolds based on the subconscious beliefs and patterns that guide your decisions, actions, and reactions every day.

What Is the Subconscious Mind?

The subconscious mind is everything you are not actively aware of. It holds all of your memories, emotions, and beliefs, some of which were formed as early as childhood. These beliefs, whether positive or negative, form the filter through which you see the world, and they shape everything from your daily decisions to your long-term goals.

Here's the kicker: Most of the beliefs that guide your life were formed long before you even realized they were there. The experiences you had growing up, the things you were told, the emotions you felt—all of these contributed to shaping your beliefs about yourself, others, and the world around you. And often, these beliefs are operating on autopilot, without you even realizing it.

How Does the Subconscious Influence Your Reality?

Now, you might be wondering, "How does this actually shape my reality?" Let me explain it in simple terms. Everything we do, think and feel is influenced by our subconscious programming. It dictates how we respond to situations, what we believe we deserve, and even how we manifest opportunities or block them.

For example, if you grew up in an environment where money was always a source of stress or scarcity, your subconscious might hold beliefs like "Money doesn't grow on trees" or "I'll never be wealthy." As a result, when opportunities for abundance present themselves, your subconscious may sabotage them. It might make you feel anxious or unworthy, preventing you from stepping into your potential.

On the flip side, if you've been raised in an environment where you were taught that you're capable, valuable, and deserving of success, your subconscious will likely support your efforts to create abundance, love, and success. You'll approach life from a place of confidence and attraction, and the universe will respond accordingly.

The Subconscious: Friend or Foe?

The tricky part is that the subconscious doesn't distinguish between what's real and what's imagined. It takes everything at face value. So, if you repeatedly tell yourself, "I'm not good enough," "I'll never be successful," or "I'm always unlucky," your subconscious will believe those things as truths and bring those experiences into your life.

That's why manifestation can feel so difficult for some people—because even if you consciously want something different (like a dream job, financial abundance, or a loving relationship), your subconscious might be running a different program. It's like trying to drive a car while the brakes are on.

But here's the good news: You can reprogram your subconscious mind. Just as you can update the software on your computer, you can update your internal beliefs and habits. And once you do that, you'll begin to see how quickly your life starts to shift.

Shifting the Subconscious: Reprogramming Your Beliefs

If you want to manifest a new reality, the first step is to become aware of your subconscious programming. This means paying attention to the beliefs and thoughts that pop up during your day, especially those related to the areas of your life you want to change. Do you have thoughts like:

- "I'll never be good enough to do that."
- "I always struggle with money."
- "It's too hard to find a partner who understands me."

If these thoughts sound familiar, don't worry—you're not alone. Everyone has subconscious beliefs that influence their reality. The key is to start identifying them and then work on shifting them.

Here's a simple exercise you can do to uncover some of your subconscious beliefs:

1. Grab a journal and set a timer for 10 minutes.
2. Write down your answers to the following prompts:
    - "Money means…"
    - "Love means…"
    - "Success means…"
    - "I am…"
3. After writing, take a moment to reflect on what came up. Do any of your answers surprise you? Are there patterns of limitation, fear, or doubt?

This exercise helps you bring awareness to the beliefs you may have carried for years. Once you can see them, you're in a position to change them.

How to Reprogram Your Subconscious for Manifestation

Reprogramming the subconscious doesn't happen overnight, but it's entirely possible with consistent practice. Here are a few techniques you can start using today:

- **Affirmations:** Repeating positive statements daily helps shift your subconscious beliefs. For example: "I am worthy of success," "Money flows to me easily and abundantly," or "I am deserving of love and happiness."
- **Visualization:** Picture yourself already living the life you want. The more vividly you imagine it, the more your subconscious begins to believe it's possible.
- **Hypnosis or Guided Meditation:** These tools allow you to enter a relaxed state where your subconscious is most receptive to new suggestions. Listening to recordings that focus on positive beliefs can be incredibly powerful.

Remember, the subconscious mind is a powerful ally when you understand how to work with it. By bringing awareness to the beliefs that shape your reality, you're already taking the first step in shifting them. As you continue to reprogram your subconscious, you'll find that manifestation becomes less about wishing for things and more about aligning your energy with the life you want to create.

In the next chapter, we'll dive deeper into how you can use the power of your emotions and energy to attract the things you desire. For now, start becoming aware of your subconscious programming—and get ready for your next breakthrough.

Understanding Mental Blocks and Limiting Beliefs

When it comes to manifestation, one of the biggest obstacles people face is the mental blocks and limiting beliefs that hold them back. These are the invisible walls that prevent you from stepping into your true potential, often without you even realizing it. But just as the subconscious mind shapes your reality, your beliefs and thought patterns directly impact what you're able to manifest.

Mental blocks are like roadblocks in your mind—they stop you from moving forward or achieving your goals. These blocks are often based on limiting beliefs you've carried with you for years, whether they were formed in childhood or built up from past experiences. Sometimes, they come from messages we've received from society, family, or even our own inner doubts.

For example, if you were raised in an environment where money was always a source of stress, you might have internalized the belief that *money is hard to come by* or that *wealth is only for certain people*. These beliefs form the foundation of your mental blocks, and they create a cycle of limitations.

What Are Limiting Beliefs?

Limiting beliefs are the stories we tell ourselves about what we are capable of or worthy of. They are often rooted in fear, self-doubt, or past experiences. These beliefs can be about anything—your abilities, your worth, your potential, or your place in the world.

A limiting belief could be as simple as:

- "I'm not good enough."
- "I'll never be successful."
- "I don't deserve love."
- "I'm not smart enough to start my own business."

These beliefs are self-imposed barriers that hold us back from pursuing our dreams. But here's the thing: Limiting beliefs are not truths. They are just thoughts—thoughts you've accepted as truth without questioning them.

Inherited Patterns: Where Do They Come From?

Another major source of mental blocks is inherited patterns, or what some people call "generational beliefs." These are the thought patterns, behaviors, and beliefs you inherit from your family, culture, or society. Think of it as the programming you get from the environment around you growing up. It's like being handed down a set of blueprints that dictate how you see the world and what you believe is possible.

For example, if your parents or caregivers often talked about "struggling to make ends meet" or had a scarcity mindset when it came to money, you may have inherited the belief that *money is scarce* and *wealth is difficult to achieve*. This inherited belief can be passed down unconsciously, and it can shape your decisions and actions as you move through life, often without you even realizing it.

Inherited patterns also show up in other areas of your life, like relationships, health, and career. If your family had a pattern of unhealthy relationships, you might unknowingly repeat those same patterns in your own life. Or if your parents always prioritized work over well-being, you might have internalized the belief that *success means sacrificing personal happiness.*

Mental blocks and limiting beliefs show up in different ways, but they all have one thing in common: they prevent you from moving forward. They often take the form of:

- **Procrastination:** You want to take action but keep putting it off, convincing yourself you'll do it later.
- **Self-sabotage:** You start making progress but somehow manage to derail your own success (often without realizing it).
- **Fear of failure:** You avoid trying new things because you're convinced you'll fail or aren't good enough.
- **Perfectionism:** You feel like you have to get everything perfect before you take action, causing you to get stuck in overthinking.
- **Imposter syndrome:** You feel like you're not truly qualified for what you want to do, so you hold yourself back from pursuing opportunities.

All of these behaviors come from deep-rooted limiting beliefs. It's important to recognize them for what they are—*signposts* that show you where your beliefs need shifting. Once you understand what's holding you back, you can take conscious steps to change it.

Before you can remove mental blocks, you need to first identify them. The good news is that they're not hidden forever. You can start by paying attention to your thought patterns, especially those related to areas where you want change—whether it's your career, relationships, or finances.

Take a moment to ask yourself:

- What's the story I've been telling myself about this area of my life?
- Do I believe that I deserve success, or do I think it's for others but not me?
- When I think about my dreams, do I feel excited, or do I feel fear or doubt?

Start journaling your thoughts and notice the recurring themes. You may be surprised at how often limiting beliefs pop up in your thinking.

Once you've identified your limiting beliefs, it's time to release them. Here are some practical ways to do so:

1. **Challenge the Beliefs:** Start questioning your limiting beliefs. Ask yourself, "Is this really true?" or "Where's the evidence for this belief?" You might find that many of your beliefs are based on outdated or false information.

   For example, if you believe that *money is hard to come by*, ask yourself, "Are there people who are wealthy and happy? How did they get there?"

2. **Reframe the Narrative:** Replace negative beliefs with positive, empowering ones. If your belief is *"I'm not good enough,"* reframe it to *"I am capable and worthy of success."* The more you affirm new beliefs, the more they will replace the old ones.

3. **Visualization:** Spend time visualizing the life you want to manifest. Imagine yourself already living that life. Feel the emotions of success, abundance, and happiness. This technique sends new messages to your subconscious and helps reprogram those old, limiting beliefs.

4. **Affirmations:** Use affirmations that directly address the limiting beliefs you're working to remove. For example, if you struggle with the belief that you're not worthy of love, repeat: *"I am deserving of love and meaningful relationships."*
5. **Energetic Healing:** Sometimes, deeply ingrained beliefs need deeper work. Techniques like Reiki, EFT (Emotional Freedom Technique), or meditation can help clear energetic blockages and reset your belief systems.

The key to manifestation is clearing the mental clutter that holds you back. Once you remove these mental blocks, limiting beliefs, and inherited patterns, you'll find that manifestation becomes much easier. As you begin to change your beliefs, you'll notice that opportunities, people, and experiences that align with your new beliefs start to show up in your life.

Remember, it's not about being perfect—it's about being aware and making small, consistent changes. With time, you'll create a new mindset that supports your dreams instead of standing in the way of them. In the next chapter, we'll explore how to align your energy with your desires to attract the life you want.

The Identity Shift – From "Hoping" to "Knowing"

The Power of Identity

When it comes to manifestation, one of the most important steps you can take is shifting your identity—who you believe you are at your core. So much of our ability to manifest stems from how we see ourselves. If you view yourself as someone who hopes for things to happen, rather than someone who knows they will, you'll be creating a gap between where you are and where you want to be.

The truth is, that you are already capable of manifesting the life you desire, but this requires a shift in your identity. It's not enough to simply wish for something. You must believe that it is already yours, deep down. When you make the shift from hoping to knowing, you unlock your full potential to create the life you desire.

Hoping vs. Knowing

Many people approach manifestation from a place of hope—they desire something, but they don't truly believe it's possible for them. Hope is a wonderful emotion, but it often comes with a sense of uncertainty. It's like saying, "I hope this works out" or "I hope I can make this happen." While hope is the first step toward belief, it's not enough to manifest the life you truly want.

When you are in the "hoping" stage, there's often an underlying fear or doubt that holds you back. You might feel like you're waiting for permission or waiting for the right circumstances to fall into place. The key difference is that in this stage, you're putting your power outside of yourself. You're hoping for things to change, rather than taking ownership of your ability to create change.

On the other hand, knowing is a state of confidence and certainty. It's not about wishing for something to happen—it's about feeling that it is already yours. When you shift to knowing, you stop questioning whether you're worthy of success or abundance. Instead, you begin to embody the mindset that whatever you desire is already in alignment with who you are. This shift is transformational because it eliminates doubt and opens you to limitless possibilities.

The identity shift from hoping to knowing is crucial for several reasons:

1. **You Take Aligned Action:** When you know that something is already on its way to you, your actions will reflect that belief. You begin to take inspired action, rather than just hoping or waiting for things to fall into place. You trust yourself and the universe, and you move forward confidently.

2. **You Stop Doubting Yourself:** Doubt is one of the greatest barriers to manifestation. When you're in a state of hope, you allow doubts to creep in. "What if this doesn't work?" "What if I'm not good enough?" When you shift to knowing, you recognize that you are already deserving and capable of creating your desires.

3. **You Attract What You Are:** Like attracts like. If you are hoping for something, you're still operating from a place of lack or uncertainty. However, when you shift to knowing, you elevate your vibration to match the energy of abundance, success, and fulfillment. This shift attracts what is already aligned with you—opportunities, people, and experiences that reflect the certainty you now have in yourself.

4. **You Stop Waiting for External Validation:** So often, we put our manifestation power in the hands of others or external circumstances. We wait for approval or confirmation before taking action. But when you know that you are the creator of your reality, you stop waiting for permission. You trust yourself, and you take inspired steps towards your goals—whether or not the world around you agrees or understands.

How to Make the Shift from Hoping to Knowing

Making the shift from hoping to knowing requires a conscious effort to change your thought patterns and beliefs. Here are some steps you can take to solidify your new identity:

1. **Step Into the Version of You Who Already Has It:**
   One of the most powerful ways to make this shift is by imagining yourself as the person who has already achieved what you desire. How would you show up in the world if you already had everything you want? How would you walk, talk, think, and act if you were already living your dream life?

   Start to embody this version of yourself in small ways. If you want to manifest a new career, begin acting like someone who is already successful in that field. If you want more love in your life, carry yourself with the confidence and openness of someone who knows they are deserving of deep, meaningful relationships.

2. **Affirmations of Knowing:**
   Affirmations are a powerful tool in shifting your identity. However, instead of affirming something you're hoping for, focus on affirmations that embody certainty. For example:
   - "I know I am worthy of all the abundance life has to offer."
   - "I am already successful, and everything I want is coming to me."
   - "I trust that the universe supports me and my desires."

Repeat these affirmations daily until they become part of your natural belief system.

3. **Visualize Your Desired Reality:**
    Visualization is one of the most effective tools for making the shift from hoping to knowing. Spend time every day visualizing yourself already living the life you want. Imagine every detail in vivid color—the sights, sounds, and feelings associated with achieving your goal.

    As you visualize, feel the certainty in your body. Don't just hope for it—know that it's already happening. This energy will align you with your desires and bring them to fruition.

4. **Release Doubt and Fear:**
    Doubt is the enemy of manifestation. Every time a fear-based thought or doubt comes up, recognize it and gently replace it with knowing. You can't eliminate doubt entirely overnight, but every time you replace doubt with knowing, you are strengthening your new identity.

5. **Take Inspired Action:**
    Knowing requires action. It's not enough to sit back and hope that your desires will manifest. When you know something is meant for you, you take action from a place of certainty and alignment. Trust your intuition and take steps toward your goals, even if they feel small at first. The more you act from a place of knowing, the more momentum you build.

When you make the shift from hoping to knowing, you not only increase your ability to manifest your desires, but you also step into a life filled with abundance, confidence, and self-trust. You will no longer feel like you're waiting for something to happen—you'll be creating your reality with every thought, action, and belief.

This shift is empowering because it allows you to take control of your life and recognize that you are the creator of your own experiences. As you embody the identity of someone who knows they are worthy of success, love, abundance, and happiness, the world around you will begin to reflect that knowing.

Chapter 2

Clarity is Power

Creating a "Vision Map" vs. a Vague Wish List

The Power of Clear Vision

Manifestation begins with clarity. Without a clear vision of what you truly desire, it's difficult to direct your energy toward it. And while many people have a wish list of things they'd like to achieve, this list is often vague, lacking the depth and clarity needed to make real progress. A wish list can leave you dreaming about your desires without actually creating a pathway to them.

On the other hand, a Vision Map is a powerful tool that turns your desires into actionable steps. It's not just about what you want; it's about how you're going to make it happen, and more importantly, it's about stepping into the identity of someone who already has what they desire.

So, let's take a look at the key differences between a vague wish list and a Vision Map, and explore how you can create one that brings your dreams to life.

What's the Difference Between a Wish List and a Vision Map?

A wish list is a simple list of things you'd like to have or achieve, such as "I want to travel more," "I want a new car," or "I want to start my own business." While this is a good start, it lacks the clarity, depth, and intentionality needed to make your desires a reality. A wish list often leaves too much to chance and doesn't give you a clear picture of how to move forward.

A Vision Map, on the other hand, is much more than just a list. It's a visual and emotional roadmap that incorporates the details of your desires and organizes them into actionable goals and steps. A Vision Map goes beyond the "what" and explores the "how" and "why." It brings your goals to life by connecting you with the emotions and identity of someone who has already achieved them.

The process of creating a Vision Map engages your imagination, your subconscious, and your conscious mind. It helps you gain clarity, overcome any mental blocks, and gives you a strong foundation to take inspired action.

Why a Vision Map Works Better Than a Wish List

1. **Clarity and Focus:** A vague wish list leaves you uncertain about what you actually want. You may know what you *don't want* or what you *wish for*, but a Vision Map forces you to define your goals clearly and specifically. The clearer you are about your desires, the easier it is to align your thoughts, feelings, and actions toward them.

2. **Actionable Steps:** A wish list doesn't provide a roadmap to achieving your goals. It may include things like "I

want to lose weight" or "I want to be more successful," but it doesn't show you how to get there. A Vision Map, however, includes actionable steps that break down big goals into smaller, manageable chunks. Each step brings you closer to manifesting your vision.

3. **Alignment with Your Highest Self:** When you create a Vision Map, you are not just setting goals; you are connecting with the version of you who already has those goals. You get clear on the identity you need to embody in order to attract your desires. This alignment with your highest self is essential for manifestation because it signals to the universe that you are ready to receive.

4. **Emotional Connection:** One of the most powerful aspects of a Vision Map is that it taps into your emotions. By visualizing what your dreams look like and how they will make you feel, you create an emotional connection that propels you forward. A wish list is often disconnected from emotion; it's a set of desires that may or may not evoke strong feelings. The emotional power behind your Vision Map gives you the energy and drive to take consistent action.

5. **Visualization and Manifestation:** Vision boards and maps are tools for visualizing your goals and dreams. Seeing your desires on paper or in images every day helps you stay focused and aligned with what you want. It reminds you to act from a place of knowing, rather than hoping and sends a clear message to your subconscious that your goals are already on their way.

Creating a Vision Map is a deeply personal process, and there's no "right" way to do it. However, there are some key steps you can follow to ensure that your Vision Map is clear, actionable, and aligned with your goals.

1. **Start with Clarity:**
   Begin by getting crystal clear on what you truly want. Write down your desires in specific terms. Instead of saying, "I want to be rich," try something more specific like, "I want to make $100,000 by the end of this year." Instead of saying, "I want to be healthier," try, "I want to be able to run 5 miles without stopping by December." The more specific you can be, the better.

   Ask yourself: What do I truly desire? What does success look like for me? What do I want to create in my life? Get detailed in your vision, and don't hold back.

2. **Identify the Steps:**
   Once you've clarified your goals, break them down into actionable steps. For each goal, ask yourself, "What needs to happen for this to become a reality?" If you want to start your own business, for example, you might list steps like:

   - Research business ideas and identify a niche.
   - Write a business plan.
   - Set a budget for startup costs.
   - Network with potential clients or partners.
   - Create a marketing strategy.

   The idea is to break down large goals into manageable steps. This prevents overwhelm and makes the process feel more achievable.

3. **Visualize the End Result:**
   What will it feel like to achieve your goals? How will you look, act, and feel? Take time to imagine yourself living your dream life. How does it feel to be in that space? Visualizing your success will help align your energy with your desires and attract them to you.

   You might create a vision board with images that represent your goals—like a new home, travel destinations, or your dream career. Cut out pictures, words, and phrases that resonate with your desired future, and arrange them in a way that feels inspiring to you.

4. **Map Out Your Identity:**
   Who do you need to become in order to manifest your vision? The identity shift from "hoping" to "knowing" is an essential part of the process, and your Vision Map should include the version of yourself who already has what you want. Write down the characteristics, behaviors, and attitudes that define your future self.

   For example, if your goal is to be a successful entrepreneur, your future self might be confident, disciplined, and resourceful. Ask yourself: How would this version of me show up every day? What habits does this person have? Incorporate these into your Vision Map as well.

5. **Review and Adjust Regularly:**
   A Vision Map isn't a one-time activity—it's something you should revisit and adjust regularly. Life changes and your goals may evolve over time. Make sure to update your Vision Map to reflect any new desires or adjustments.

A Vision Map doesn't work by simply creating it once and then forgetting about it. To manifest your desires, you must revisit them often. Whether it's through daily visualization, affirmations, or action, keep your Vision Map alive in your thoughts and actions. The more consistent you are, the more likely your desires will manifest.

A Vision Map is more than just a wish list—it's a powerful tool that turns your dreams into a reality. By creating a clear, detailed map of where you want to go and aligning yourself with the identity of someone who already has what they desire, you set yourself up for success. With clarity, actionable steps, and a deep emotional connection to your goals, your Vision Map becomes a roadmap to manifesting the life you've always dreamed of.

How to Ask the Universe Clearly

The Power of Asking Clearly

When it comes to manifestation, one of the most important steps is learning how to ask the Universe clearly for what you want. It's easy to wish for things, but true manifestation requires clarity, intention, and understanding that the Universe responds to specific, focused desires. The more clearly you ask, the more the Universe can align with your energy to bring you what you seek.

Think of it this way: When you make a wish, it's like sending out a signal. The clearer that signal is, the easier it is for the Universe to pick it up and respond. On the other hand, if your request is vague or uncertain, it's like trying to tune into a radio station with static—it's much harder to get a clear reception.

The good news? You have the ability to ask with precision. By getting clear on what you want, aligning your energy with it, and asking in the right way, you create a strong connection with the Universe. When this connection is made, it sets the wheels of manifestation in motion.

Why Clarity Matters in Manifestation

Clarity is essential when asking the Universe because the more specific and detailed you are, the more aligned your actions, thoughts, and feelings will be with your desires. Here's why clarity is so important:

1. **The Universe Responds to Energy:** Everything in the Universe is energy, including your thoughts and desires. If you send out unclear or mixed signals, the Universe responds with a similar level of confusion. When you ask with clarity, your energy becomes focused, and the Universe can match that energy, helping you attract what you desire.

2. **It Eliminates Doubt and Confusion:** Asking with clarity helps you eliminate the fog of doubt and uncertainty. When you know exactly what you want and why you want it, there's no room for indecision or second-guessing. This confidence sends a strong signal to the Universe that you are ready to receive what you're asking for.

3. **It Aligns Your Thoughts, Actions, and Beliefs:** Clear asking isn't just about words—it's about creating an inner alignment between your thoughts, actions, and beliefs. When you ask for something specific, you are naturally inclined to take steps that align with that goal, ensuring that the Universe can work through you and with you to bring your desires to fruition.

4. **Focus and Intent:** The more focused and intentional you are with your desires, the more the Universe will bring them into your reality. Clarity creates a powerful focal point that helps you stay aligned with your goals, guiding your decisions and actions in a way that supports manifestation.

Steps to Ask the Universe Clearly

Now that you understand why clarity is crucial, let's explore how to actually ask the Universe in a clear and powerful way. These steps will help you get into alignment with your desires and communicate with the Universe in a way that ensures your intentions are received loud and clear.

1. Get Clear on What You Want

Before you can ask for something, you must know exactly what it is you want. This step is all about specificity. The more precise you can be, the more power you bring to your request. For example, if you want to manifest a new job, don't just say, "I want a new job." Instead, get clear about the type of job you want, the salary range, the work environment, the company culture, and how it makes you feel.

Here's an exercise to help you get clear:

- Take out a journal and write down exactly what you want. Describe your desire in as much detail as possible. Be specific about every aspect of it—where it is, who's involved, how it feels, when you want it, etc.
- Ask yourself: How will my life be different once I have this? Focus on the emotions and experiences associated with your desire.

- If you have several desires, get clear on one thing at a time so you can focus your energy on each goal individually.

2. Use Present Tense Language

When you ask the Universe, it's important to frame your request as though your desire is already happening or has already manifested. The Universe works in present tense energy, so speaking in the present moment helps align your energy with what's already on its way to you.

Instead of saying, "I want to be wealthy," say something like, "I am enjoying financial abundance and freedom in my life right now."

By shifting to present tense language, you immediately send a signal that you are already in alignment with your desire. It's a subtle but powerful shift in energy that helps reinforce the belief that what you desire is already yours.

3. Ask with Gratitude

Gratitude is a magnetic energy that draws more of what you want toward you. When you ask the Universe for something, always include a feeling of gratitude in your request. Gratitude not only shifts your energy but also helps you align with the emotions of already having what you want.

For example:

- Instead of saying, "I want a new car," say, "I am so grateful for the beautiful, reliable car I now have. I feel so free and empowered driving it every day."

- Instead of "I need more money," say, "I am deeply thankful for the abundance I am attracting into my life. I feel so at peace with my financial flow."

By infusing your request with gratitude, you create an energetic match to your desires, which makes them more likely to manifest.

4. Be Specific About the "How" and the "Why"

While it's not necessary to control how your desires will unfold (the Universe works in mysterious ways), it's helpful to understand why you want something and how you want it to feel. The "why" creates emotional clarity, and the "how" connects your mind to the practical aspects of manifestation.

For example, if you want to manifest a new job:

- Why do you want this job? Think about the deeper reasons, like having more financial freedom, doing work you love, or having a better work-life balance.
- How do you want to feel in this job? Do you want to feel empowered, fulfilled, or appreciated? Focus on the emotions you want to experience, and let that guide your request.

When you know why you want something and how you want it to feel, you create a powerful emotional foundation for your request. The Universe then aligns with this energy and brings you opportunities and circumstances that match your desires.

5. Trust and Let Go

Once you've asked clearly, the next step is to trust that the Universe will deliver. Doubt and worry are the enemies of manifestation. When you ask for something and then continuously worry about how it will happen, you create resistance. Instead, trust that your desire is already on its way.

One of the most powerful things you can do is let go of the "how" and trust that the Universe knows the best way to bring your desire to you. Let go of control, and allow space for the Universe to work its magic.

The Importance of Consistency and Alignment

Asking clearly isn't a one-time thing; it's about maintaining consistent focus and alignment. Regularly revisit your desires, ask for them with clarity, and keep your energy aligned with the feeling of having already received them. Practice visualization, gratitude, and affirmations daily to stay connected to your intention and continue sending out a clear signal to the Universe.

Asking the Universe clearly is one of the most powerful steps you can take in the manifestation process. It's not just about making wishes—it's about being specific, present, and intentional with your desires. By gaining clarity, using present-tense language, expressing gratitude, and letting go of doubt, you open yourself up to receiving all the abundance and opportunities that are already on their way to you.

Remember: The Universe is always listening—so speak clearly, with intention, and trust that your desires are being fulfilled.

Practical Exercise: Write Your Personal Manifesto

What is a Personal Manifesto?

A Personal Manifesto is a powerful statement that reflects your values, goals, beliefs, and desires. It's a declaration of who you are, who you are becoming, and what you are committed to manifesting in your life. In essence, a manifesto is your personal roadmap to living the life you desire, based on clarity, intention, and alignment with your highest self.

The act of writing a manifesto is more than just jotting down a list of goals. It's about crafting a document that resonates deeply with your inner truth and expresses your commitment to living your most authentic life. It's a declaration of who you are right now, who you want to become, and the steps you are willing to take to align with your dreams.

Your manifesto serves as a guide—something you can return to whenever you feel uncertain or need to reignite your motivation. It's a way of ensuring that your thoughts, actions, and energy are always aligned with your vision, empowering you to stay focused on what truly matters.

Why Writing a Personal Manifesto is Powerful

1. **Clarity and Focus:** Writing a manifesto forces you to get clear on what truly matters to you. It's not just about the goals you want to achieve; it's about understanding the bigger picture—the values, beliefs, and feelings that drive your desires. This clarity keeps you focused and aligned with your true purpose.

2. **Commitment to Your Vision:** A manifesto is not a passive wish list—it's an active commitment. When you write your manifesto, you are affirming your intention to pursue your desires, no matter what. It helps you stay accountable to your vision and reminds you of the steps you need to take to manifest it.

3. **Empowerment and Alignment:** Writing your manifesto is an empowering experience. It helps you take ownership of your life and reminds you of the strength within you to create the life you desire. It aligns your thoughts, beliefs, and actions with your goals, making manifestation easier and more powerful.

4. **A Source of Inspiration:** A personal manifesto serves as a source of inspiration during challenging times. It can reignite your passion when things aren't going as planned and serve as a reminder of why you're on this journey in the first place.

Now that you understand the power of a Personal Manifesto, let's go over the steps to create one that is deeply meaningful and inspiring. Follow the steps below, and take your time with each one. Your manifesto is a living document that evolves with you, so don't feel the need to rush. Let it unfold naturally.

1. Define Your Core Values

Your manifesto should start by identifying what truly matters to you. These are your core values—the guiding principles that shape your decisions, actions, and interactions with the world. These values are what you stand for, and they give you a solid foundation upon which to build your vision.

To get started:

- Ask yourself: What do I believe in? What qualities do I admire in others? What would I stand up for, no matter what?
- Write down 5-10 core values that resonate with you, such as honesty, growth, love, abundance, peace, creativity, courage, or freedom.
- Reflect on how these values align with your current life and how they can shape your future.

Example:

"My core values are love, growth, authenticity, and gratitude. I believe in the power of kindness, the importance of learning, and living true to myself."

2. Envision Your Ideal Life

Your manifesto should be a reflection of your vision for your future. This is your opportunity to get clear on your desires—whether they're related to relationships, career, health, or personal development.

To do this:

- Visualize your ideal life in detail. What does it look like? How do you feel in this life? What are you doing? Who are you surrounded by?
- Describe your vision in terms of feelings, not just things. For example, instead of just saying "I want a successful career," describe the emotions you associate with success: "I feel empowered, fulfilled, and confident in my work."

Example:

"I see myself traveling the world, writing books, and living in a home filled with light and love. I am deeply connected with my family and friends, and my work allows me to express my creativity while making a positive impact on others."

3. Write Your Affirmations

Affirmations are powerful statements that affirm your belief in yourself and your ability to achieve your desires. When you write your manifesto, include affirmations that reflect your new identity -the person you are becoming.

To craft your affirmations:

- Write in the present tense, as if you are already living your desired reality.
- Use positive, empowering language.
- Incorporate both general and specific affirmations about who you are and what you're creating in your life.

Example:

"I am a confident, successful writer. I trust my intuition and take inspired action every day. I am worthy of abundance, and I receive it with gratitude."

4. Include Your Commitments

A Personal Manifesto is not just about what you want—it's also about what you are willing to do to make it happen. Include a section where you commit to taking consistent, aligned action toward your goals.

To write your commitments:

- Reflect on what actions you need to take to align with your vision. What steps can you take today that will bring you closer to your desired future?
- Focus on small, consistent actions rather than overwhelming yourself with big leaps. Manifestation is a process, and every step counts.

Example:

"I commit to waking up each day with gratitude and a clear intention for how I will move toward my goals. I will take at least one action every day that brings me closer to my vision."

5. Incorporate Gratitude and Affirm Your Faith

A Personal Manifesto is incomplete without gratitude and trust. Manifestation requires both gratitude for what you already have and faith in the process. The Universe is always working on your behalf, and expressing your gratitude and trust strengthens the connection.

To add gratitude and faith:

- Write a section that acknowledges everything you are grateful for in your life right now. Focus on the abundance, love, and opportunities that are already present.
- Affirm your trust in the Universe's timing and your belief in your ability to manifest your desires.

Example:

"I am deeply grateful for the love, abundance, and opportunities that surround me. I trust the Universe is guiding me toward my highest good, and I believe in my ability to manifest everything I desire."

6. Review and Refine Your Manifesto Regularly

Your Personal Manifesto is not a static document—it's something you should revisit regularly. Over time, you may find that your desires evolve or that your vision shifts as you grow and change. Make a habit of reading your manifesto every day to reinforce your alignment with your goals.

As you review your manifesto:

- Take note of how it makes you feel. Does it inspire you? Does it excite you? If not, tweak it to better reflect your evolving desires.
- Add new affirmations, commitments, or sections as needed. Your manifesto is meant to grow with you.

Writing your Personal Manifesto is one of the most powerful acts you can take in the manifestation process. It's a declaration of your intentions, your desires, and your commitment to becoming the person you are destined to be. By writing it with clarity, intention, and love, you create a powerful document that will guide you on your journey toward manifesting the life of your dreams.

Remember, your manifesto is a living, breathing document that evolves with you. Read it often, add to it, and allow it to inspire you as you take bold steps toward your highest potential.

Chapter 3

Energy and Emotion: The Frequency Factor

Vibrations Explained (Emotions = Energy in Motion)

The Science of Vibrations

Everything in the Universe is energy—every thought, every feeling, every object. This energy vibrates at different frequencies, creating a web of interconnected forces that shape our reality. The concept of vibrations isn't just metaphysical; it's rooted in science. Quantum physics tells us that at the most fundamental level, everything is made of energy, and energy moves in waves, vibrating at different speeds.

The same principle applies to human beings. We are made up of energy, and our thoughts, feelings, and emotions all carry their own unique vibrational frequency. The energy we emit—through our thoughts, words, and actions—sends out signals to the Universe, attracting experiences that match our frequency. Essentially, what we feel determines the energy we emit, and the energy we emit determines the experiences we attract.

When you hear someone say, "You're vibrating at a high frequency" or "You need to raise your vibration," they are talking about the energy you are putting out into the world through your emotions. It's important to understand that emotions are energy in motion, and they have the power to either attract or repel experiences in your life.

Emotions are not just intangible feelings; they are vibrational frequencies that flow through us. Think of them as waves of energy moving through your body, influencing your mental and physical state. Each emotion, whether it's joy, fear, love, or anger, has a unique frequency.

For example:

- **Love, gratitude, and joy** vibrate at high frequencies. These emotions are expansive and attract positive experiences, people, and opportunities into your life.
- **Fear, anger, and jealousy** vibrate at lower frequencies. These emotions are constrictive and tend to attract experiences that mirror their energy, often leading to feelings of frustration or dissatisfaction.

The key idea here is that your emotions act as signals to the Universe, creating a feedback loop. When you feel joy and love, you send out a signal of high frequency, which then attracts experiences that match this vibration. On the other hand, when you experience negative emotions, your frequency drops, and the Universe responds accordingly.

The Emotional Scale and Its Impact on Your Vibration

To understand how different emotions influence your vibration, it's helpful to look at the emotional scale. This scale ranges from low-frequency emotions like despair and fear to high-frequency emotions like peace and love. Every emotion you experience can be placed somewhere along this scale, and your goal is to consciously move toward higher vibrations for the most positive manifestations.

Here's a breakdown of the emotional scale:

1. **Low Frequency:**
   - **Fear, Grief, Despair, Guilt, Shame**: These emotions vibrate at very low frequencies and can feel draining. They often create a sense of limitation or resistance in your life. The energy behind these emotions is dense, and when you dwell in them, you attract situations that reinforce negativity.

2. **Medium Frequency:**
   - **Anger, Frustration, Worry, Doubt**: These emotions have a slightly higher frequency but still come from a place of resistance. They don't have the expansive quality of higher-vibrating emotions, but they are more powerful than low-frequency emotions. Often, these emotions are related to a desire for change or a response to an external circumstance.

3. **High Frequency:**
   - **Love, Joy, Gratitude, Peace, and Empowerment:** These emotions vibrate at very high frequencies. They come from a place of abundance, connection, and alignment. When you operate from these emotions, you send out a signal that is expansive and magnetic. These are the emotions that attract miracles, opportunities, and experiences that reflect your inner harmony.

How to Raise Your Vibration

Now that we understand the emotional scale and how different emotions correspond to different vibrational frequencies, the next step is to learn how to raise our vibration. Raising your vibration involves shifting your emotional state to higher frequencies so you can attract positive, aligned experiences.

Here are some practical steps you can take to raise your vibration:

1. **Practice Gratitude:** Gratitude is one of the most powerful ways to elevate your vibration. When you focus on what you're grateful for, you immediately shift your energy from lack to abundance, from negative to positive. Make a habit of listing things you're grateful for every day.

2. **Engage in Activities that Bring You Joy:** Do things that make you feel good—whether it's listening to your favorite music, dancing, meditating, spending time with loved ones, or engaging in creative pursuits. The more you engage in activities that uplift your spirit, the higher your vibration will be.

3. **Meditate:** Meditation is a powerful tool for calming your mind and connecting with your inner self. It allows you to release negative emotions and clear your mind of limiting beliefs. By practicing mindfulness or guided meditation, you can shift your energy and achieve a higher state of consciousness.

4. **Affirmations:** Positive affirmations are a simple but effective way to raise your vibration. By affirming things like "I am worthy of love and abundance," "I am in alignment with my highest good," and "I am a magnet for positivity," you send out a high-vibrational energy that draws those very things into your life.

5. **Surround Yourself with Positive People and Environments:** The energy of the people you interact with can significantly affect your vibration. Spend time with those who uplift and inspire you, and avoid toxic environments or relationships that drain your energy. Surrounding yourself with positivity helps you maintain a higher frequency.

6. **Release Negative Emotions:** Instead of holding on to anger, fear, or resentment, make a conscious effort to release them. You can do this through journaling, breathwork, or simply allowing yourself to feel and process the emotion without attaching to it. The quicker you let go of negative emotions, the easier it is to maintain a high vibration.

Emotions are not just random feelings that come and go—they are the energy that shapes your reality. Understanding that emotions are energy in motion allows you to take control of your vibrational frequency and consciously align yourself with the life you want to manifest.

By learning to raise your vibration and maintain high-frequency emotions like love, gratitude, and joy, you will attract experiences that reflect those energies. Remember, the Universe responds to your energy, so make sure the energy you put out into the world is a reflection of the life you want to create.

Start today by paying attention to how you feel, and make choices that elevate your emotional state. Your vibration is your compass—it guides you toward your desires and helps you create a reality that reflects your highest potential.

How to Align Your Frequency with Your Desires

Understanding the Need for Alignment

The Law of Attraction teaches us that like attracts like. The energy or frequency you emit into the Universe directly influences what you attract back. If you're feeling fear, doubt, or frustration, you're sending out a low-frequency signal that will attract more of the same. On the other hand, if you are vibrating with love, joy, abundance, and gratitude, you will attract experiences that mirror these high-frequency emotions.

The key to effective manifestation lies in alignment—not just wishing for something, but aligning your energy with the frequency of that thing. When you are in harmony with your desires, the Universe effortlessly flows towards you, drawing your dreams into your reality.

So, how do you align your frequency with your desires? Let's break it down.

Step 1: Get Clear on What You Truly Want

Alignment begins with clarity. You can't align with a desire if you aren't sure what it is. This first step requires you to dive deep and ask yourself, "What do I truly want?" Your desires must come from a place of authenticity, not what you think you "should" want or what others expect of you. Your desires should come from your heart, from your soul's true calling.

Take time to reflect on your life, your values, and your long-term vision. What excites you? What lights you up? Is it a thriving career, a loving relationship, improved health, or financial freedom? Once you know what you truly desire, it becomes easier to set the intention to align with it.

Step 2: Shift Your Focus from Lack to Abundance

A critical part of aligning your frequency is shifting from a mindset of lack to one of abundance. When you focus on what's missing in your life, you are vibrating at a lower frequency. This mindset perpetuates feelings of scarcity, which in turn attracts more of the same.

To align your frequency with your desires, focus on what you already have—the abundance in your life right now. Recognize the love, opportunities, health, and joy that are already present, no matter how small they may seem. This shift in focus brings you into a state of gratitude and opens the door to attracting more of what you want.

Start with a daily gratitude practice. Acknowledge all the good things in your life and celebrate them. By doing so, you raise your vibrational frequency and begin to align with abundance.

Step 3: Cultivate the Emotions of Your Desire

Your emotions are the direct manifestation of your vibration. If you want to attract abundance, you must feel abundant. If you want love, you must feel loved. The key is to embody the emotions that your desired outcome would naturally evoke, even before the physical manifestation has arrived.

To align your frequency with your desires, take time to cultivate the emotions that align with your vision. Visualize yourself already living your desires and allow the emotions of joy, gratitude, excitement, or peace to fill your body. Let these positive emotions flow through you. The more you can stay in these elevated emotions, the more you will vibrate at the frequency of your desires.

For example:

- If you want financial abundance, imagine the freedom you'd feel with money flowing easily into your life. Feel the excitement of being able to live your dream life without worry.
- If you want a loving relationship, visualize the warmth and connection you'd experience with your ideal partner. Feel the love, compassion, and joy that would fill your life.

By consistently feeling the emotions of your desires, you program your body and mind to align with the frequency that attracts those desires.

Step 4: Take Inspired Action

Alignment doesn't just happen by thinking or feeling positive thoughts. Action is a critical component of the manifestation process. However, it's important to recognize that the action you take should come from a place of inspiration, not pressure or force. This is where the concept of inspired action comes into play.

Inspired action is an action that feels natural, exciting, and effortless. It is a response to your inner guidance. When you align your frequency with your desires, you'll begin to feel intuitive nudges or ideas that lead you to take action toward your goals.

For example, if you desire a new job, inspired action might be updating your resume or sending out a few applications. If you're manifesting a better lifestyle, it might look like choosing healthier meals or finding a workout routine that excites you. These actions come from a place of inspiration, rather than desperation.

Trust yourself and follow the guidance that comes from your intuition. Your aligned actions will magnetize your desires into your life with ease.

Step 5: Trust the Universe's Timing

One of the most important aspects of alignment is trust. Trust that the Universe is always working in your favor, even when things don't seem to be happening as quickly as you'd like. Trust that everything is unfolding exactly as it should, and that the Universe has a perfect plan for you.

It's common to feel impatience or doubt when you're waiting for your desires to manifest. However, impatience often comes from a place of misalignment. When you align your frequency with your desires, you don't have to force or rush things. You trust that what is meant for you will come to you in perfect timing.

To stay in trust:

- Let go of attachment to how and when your desires will manifest. Detach from the outcome and focus on the process of aligning with your desires.
- Practice patience. Remind yourself that the Universe is always moving things around behind the scenes to bring you what you want.

Step 6: Remove Resistance

Resistance is anything that blocks the flow of energy between you and your desires. This can come in the form of limiting beliefs, fear, negative self-talk, or past experiences that make you doubt your worthiness.

To align with your desires, you must clear any resistance standing in your way. Start by identifying your limiting beliefs. Are you telling yourself that you aren't worthy of success or love? Are you holding onto the idea that money is hard to come by?

Once you identify resistance, consciously choose to release it. You can do this through affirmations, visualization, or even by seeking help from a coach or therapist. Let go of fear and doubt, and replace those thoughts with empowering beliefs that support your manifestation journey.

Step 7: Practice Self-Love and Self-Worth

A big part of alignment comes from feeling worthy of your desires. If you don't believe you deserve the life you want, your frequency will remain misaligned. You must cultivate a strong sense of self-love and self-worth in order to align with your desires.

Start by affirming your worth every day. Remind yourself that you are deserving of all the abundance, love, and success you desire. Engage in self-care practices that honor and nurture yourself. The more you love and respect yourself, the easier it will be to align with the vibration of your desires.

Aligning your frequency with your desires is not a one-time act; it's a continuous practice. It requires conscious attention to your thoughts, emotions, and actions. The more you can cultivate a high vibrational state and stay in alignment with your desires, the more you will experience the effortless manifestation of those desires in your life.

Remember, manifestation is a dance between clarity, trust, inspired action, and belief in your own worth. By following the steps outlined in this chapter, you'll be on your way to creating a life that is truly aligned with your deepest desires.

Emotional Mastery Techniques (EFT, Breathwork, Visualization)

Why Emotional Mastery Matters

Emotional mastery is one of the most powerful tools you can possess in your journey toward manifestation and personal growth. Your emotions are your guiding compass—they signal whether you are in alignment with your desires or whether you are allowing limiting beliefs and resistance to take over. Learning to master your emotions means taking control of your inner world, allowing you to consciously direct your energy toward the life you desire.

In this chapter, we'll explore three key emotional mastery techniques: EFT (Emotional Freedom Techniques),

Breathwork, and Visualization. Each of these tools allows you to release negative emotions, shift your state of being, and align your vibration with your highest desires.

Let's dive into how these techniques work and how you can use them to create emotional balance and empowerment.

1. Emotional Freedom Techniques (EFT)

EFT, commonly known as tapping, is a powerful tool for emotional mastery that combines elements of acupressure and psychological techniques. It's based on the premise that negative emotions and unresolved issues are a result of disruptions in the body's energy system. By tapping on specific meridian points on the body while addressing the emotional issue at hand, EFT helps restore balance to the body's energy, allowing for emotional healing and clarity.

How EFT Works

EFT targets the energy meridians in the body, similar to acupuncture but without the use of needles. The process involves tapping on key points on the head, face, and upper body while focusing on the issue or emotion you wish to release. As you tap, you combine physical tapping with verbal affirmations that address the emotional disturbance, which can help to clear negative energy and shift your emotional state.

The Basic Tapping Points Include:

1. Top of the head – crown of the head
2. Eyebrow – where the eyebrow meets the nose
3. Side of the eye – on the bone next to the outer eye corner

4. Under the eye – on the bone beneath the eye
5. Under the nose – above the upper lip
6. Chin – in the indentation between the chin and lower lip
7. Collarbone – where the collarbone meets the sternum
8. Under the arm – about 4 inches below the armpit

Using EFT for Emotional Mastery

When you experience negative emotions such as fear, anger, or doubt, EFT can help you release them and shift your vibration. The process involves:

1. Identifying the emotion or belief you want to release. For example, "I feel unworthy of love."
2. Rating the intensity of the emotion on a scale from 1 to 10 to gauge how strong the emotion is.
3. Tapping through the meridian points while repeating affirmations that acknowledge the emotion without judgment. For instance: "Even though I feel unworthy of love, I deeply and completely accept myself."
4. Reassessing the emotion after tapping to see if the intensity has decreased. Repeat the process until the emotional charge around the issue dissipates.

By regularly using EFT, you can start to reprogram your mind, shift negative thought patterns, and clear emotional blockages that have been holding you back from manifesting your desires.

2. Breathwork

Breathwork is a powerful practice that involves using your breath to bring balance and clarity to your mind and body.

Through focused and intentional breathing, you can reduce stress, release stored emotions, and increase your vibration to a higher state of alignment.

Why Breathwork Works

Our breath is the bridge between our conscious and unconscious mind. When we are stressed, anxious, or fearful, we tend to breathe shallowly, activating the body's "fight or flight" response. By consciously controlling our breath, we activate the parasympathetic nervous system, which helps to relax the body and mind, reducing stress and anxiety. Breathwork also brings more oxygen into the body, helping to clear mental fog and connect you with your inner state of peace.

Simple Breathwork Techniques for Emotional Mastery

Here are a few breathwork techniques that can help you control your emotions and align your frequency with your desires:

1. **Deep Belly Breathing:**
   This technique involves taking slow, deep breaths that fill your lungs from the bottom up. As you inhale, focus on expanding your belly (not just your chest), and as you exhale, allow the breath to leave your body slowly. Deep belly breathing helps calm the nervous system and shift your emotional state from stress to relaxation.

How to do it:

- Sit or lie down comfortably.
- Place one hand on your belly and the other on your chest.

- Inhale deeply through your nose for a count of four, allowing your belly to expand.
- Exhale slowly through your mouth for a count of six, allowing your belly to contract.
- Repeat for 5–10 minutes, focusing on deepening your breath.

2. **Box Breathing (Square Breathing):**
Box breathing helps balance your energy and brings you back into the present moment. It involves inhaling, holding, exhaling, and holding the breath again for equal counts. This practice can help you break the cycle of anxious thoughts and bring emotional clarity.

How to do it:

- Inhale deeply through your nose for a count of four.
- Hold your breath for a count of four.
- Exhale slowly through your mouth for a count of four.
- Hold your breath again for a count of four.
- Repeat for 5–10 minutes.

By incorporating breathwork into your daily practice, you can create a deep sense of inner peace, release emotional tension, and elevate your vibration to align with your desires.

3. Visualization

Visualization is one of the most powerful tools you can use to master your emotions and manifest your desires. When you visualize, you are essentially programming your mind and emotions to experience what you desire in advance, which shifts your vibrational frequency to match that of your desired outcome.

How Visualization Works

Visualization involves creating vivid mental images of your goals, imagining every detail of the experience as if it has already manifested. When you can vividly imagine yourself living your dream life—feeling the emotions, seeing the sights, hearing the sounds—you create a powerful vibrational match to your desires. This emotional and mental rehearsal sends a clear signal to the Universe that you are ready to receive.

Visualization for Emotional Mastery

To effectively use visualization for emotional mastery, follow these steps:

1. **Relax and clear your mind**: Find a quiet space, close your eyes, and take a few deep breaths to center yourself.

2. **Visualize your desired outcome**: Imagine yourself living the life you want. See the details clearly—where are you? What are you doing? Who are you with? What does success feel like?

3. **Engage all of your senses**: The more real you can make the visualization feel, the more powerful the emotional shift will be. Allow yourself to experience the joy, satisfaction, and excitement that come with the manifestation.

4. **Anchor the feeling**: As you feel these positive emotions, anchor them in your body. Take note of the sensations—your heart rate, your energy levels, your feelings of peace or excitement. The more you tap into these emotions, the more you align with them.

Visualizing your desires regularly helps reprogram your mind to focus on what you want, rather than what you don't want, and reinforces a high vibrational frequency.

Emotional mastery is an ongoing process. Techniques like EFT, breathwork, and visualization empower you to shift your emotions quickly, reclaim your inner balance, and align your frequency with your desires. By incorporating these practices into your daily routine, you can clear emotional blockages, release resistance, and maintain a high-vibrational state that attracts the life you desire.

Remember, the more you practice emotional mastery, the more control you'll have over your emotional state. And when you control your emotions, you control your vibrational frequency—leading to the effortless manifestation of your dreams.

Chapter 4

The Law of Attraction Explained (Without the Fluff)

What It Really Is

The Law of Attraction (LOA) is one of the most popular concepts in the self-help and manifestation world, but it's also one of the most misunderstood. At its core, the Law of Attraction simply states: "Like attracts like."

What does that mean? It means that the energy you put out into the world—whether through your thoughts, feelings, or actions—will attract similar energy back to you. In other words, your vibrational frequency determines what you draw into your life.

Here's the key point: The Law of Attraction isn't about wishful thinking or hoping for things to magically appear. It's about understanding that you are constantly emitting energy and that energy is shaping your experiences. When you align your energy with your desires, you begin to attract opportunities, people, and circumstances that support the life you want to create.

At its simplest, the Law of Attraction is a principle of cause and effect. You are the cause, and your thoughts and emotions are the effects that radiate into the Universe. This is why it's often said that "what you think, you create."

What It Isn't

There's a lot of fluff surrounding the Law of Attraction, especially in the popular media. Many people are led to believe that it's some kind of "wishful thinking"—that if you simply visualize what you want, it will automatically manifest in your life. This is a huge misconception.

1. It's Not a Magical Wish-Granting Tool

The Law of Attraction is not about just thinking or visualizing your desires and sitting back, expecting the Universe to do the rest. It's not about *wishful thinking* where you dream of a new car and it appears in your driveway without any action or effort on your part. The Universe doesn't simply give you things because you want them or because you ask for them.

While visualization and positive thinking play a role, you must take inspired action toward your goals. The Law of Attraction is about aligning your energy with what you want, but it requires you to meet the Universe halfway. It's like a magnet—you don't just sit there waiting for the metal to come to you; you have to bring the magnet to the metal. Action is necessary for manifestation.

2. It's Not Just About Positive Thinking

Many people believe that the Law of Attraction only works if you stay positive 24/7. But this isn't true. While maintaining a positive mindset does help to raise your vibration, the Law of Attraction works based on the overall frequency of your emotions, not just your thoughts. Your feelings, beliefs, and subconscious programming are just as important as your conscious thoughts.

Negative emotions, doubts, and limiting beliefs also send out energy. If you're constantly battling with negative thought patterns or feelings of unworthiness, those too will attract experiences that match that energy, regardless of how much you "think positively."

Instead of simply trying to think positive thoughts, focus on feeling good. Your emotions are the true guidance system that determines the frequency you're putting out.

3. It's Not a Quick-Fix for Immediate Results

Another common misconception is that the Law of Attraction provides instant results. Many people get frustrated when their desires don't manifest overnight. The truth is, that manifestation is a process, not an event. It's about consistent alignment with your desires over time.

Manifestation often requires patience and trust. Just like planting a seed in the soil, you can't rush the growing process. The Universe is always working behind the scenes, arranging people, opportunities, and circumstances in your favor. But it's essential to trust the process and stay aligned with your vision—even when things don't seem to be happening right away.

How to Make the Law of Attraction Work for You

Now that we've cleared up what the Law of Attraction isn't, let's talk about how to make it work for you.

1. Focus on Your Energy, Not Just Your Thoughts

Your energy is the key to attracting what you want. It's not enough to just repeat affirmations or visualize your desires—if your underlying energy isn't aligned, you'll find it difficult to manifest. The key is to shift your emotional state to one of alignment with your desires.

When you feel good, you are naturally emitting a high-frequency vibration that aligns with the energy of your goals. This is why it's important to take the time to consciously feel the emotions you want to experience when your desires manifest. What does success feel like? What does love feel like? What does abundance feel like? Tune into those feelings daily.

2. Clarify Your Desires

The clearer you are about what you want, the easier it is to manifest it. The Universe cannot deliver vague desires. Instead of saying, "I want to be rich," be specific: "I want to earn $100,000 a year doing something I love." When you get clear on what you want, you set a focused intention that aligns your energy with your goal. Specificity is key.

3. Let Go of Attachment

One of the most important aspects of the Law of Attraction is detachment. This doesn't mean you stop wanting your desires, but it means you stop obsessing over them. When you are overly attached to a specific outcome, you're actually sending out the energy of lack and desperation—neither of which are high-frequency emotions.

Instead, trust that what you desire is already on its way. Release control and allow the Universe to deliver it in the perfect way and timing. This will help you avoid frustration and impatience, which are low-vibration emotions that only slow down the manifestation process.

4. Take Inspired Action

Manifestation is a co-creative process. You don't just wait for things to fall into your lap; you need to be actively engaged in the process. Pay attention to the intuitive nudges, ideas, and opportunities that come your way. These are signs that the Universe is guiding you toward your desires.

5. Practice Gratitude

Gratitude is one of the highest-vibration emotions you can feel. The more grateful you are for what you already have, the more you invite into your life. Gratitude helps you to stay in alignment with your desires and increases your ability to manifest more of what you want.

The Law of Attraction isn't about magic or wishful thinking. It's a simple universal principle: like attracts like. When you align your thoughts, emotions, and actions with your desires, you become a magnet for the experiences you want to create.

By understanding that manifestation requires emotional alignment, focused intention, inspired action, and trust in the process, you can begin to harness the true power of the Law of Attraction. It's not about hoping something will happen; it's about knowing it's already on its way.

Manifestation is not some mystical, unattainable power—it's a natural law of the Universe that you can use to your advantage. By aligning your energy with your desires and staying open to the flow of abundance, you unlock the full potential of the Law of Attraction.

What is the Vibrational Match System?

At the heart of the Law of Attraction lies the Vibrational Match System. Simply put, this system refers to the way that your vibration aligns with the energy of what you desire to manifest. In the simplest terms, it's like tuning an instrument. Just as a guitar string vibrates at a certain frequency, so too do you vibrate at a frequency that matches the energy of your thoughts, feelings, and actions.

In the context of manifestation, the Vibrational Match System is all about being in alignment with the things you want to attract. If you are focused on creating a particular outcome—whether it's more money, love, health, or success—you must match your vibration to that desired outcome. This means adjusting your thoughts, feelings, and energy to align with what you want to receive from the Universe.

How the Vibrational Match System Works

The Universe operates on the principle of vibration. Every thought, emotion, and action you take sends out an energetic signal into the world. Whether you realize it or not, you're constantly emitting vibrations that attract similar frequencies back to you. The Vibrational Match System is the process that dictates whether or not your energy is aligned with what you want to manifest.

Let's break this down:

- **Thoughts and Beliefs**: Your thoughts are powerful vibrational signals. If you believe that you deserve abundance, your mind will align with opportunities that bring wealth into your life. If you constantly think about what's lacking in your life, you'll attract more experiences of lack.

- **Emotions**: Your emotions are equally important in the Vibrational Match System. Positive emotions such as love, joy, and gratitude emit a high-frequency vibration, which attracts similarly high-vibration experiences. Negative emotions, on the other hand, lower your frequency and can attract experiences that mirror those low vibrations.

- **Actions**: Actions are an essential part of the equation. You can't just sit back and wait for your desires to fall into your lap. Your actions must also be in alignment with your goals. When you take inspired action—an action that feels good and in harmony with your desires—you send out the right energetic signal to the Universe, making you a perfect vibrational match for what you want.

The key to manifesting what you want is aligning your internal energy with the frequency of your desires. So, how do you align with what you want?

1. **Clarify Your Desires**: In order to align with something, you need to know what it is. Be specific about what you want. For example, if you want to manifest a new job, don't just wish for "a better job." Specify what kind of job, the salary, the benefits, the location—everything that resonates with your ideal scenario. When you clarify your

desires, you can better attune your energy to match that specific vibration.

2. **Feel the Emotions**: Manifestation is not just about thinking about what you want; it's about feeling it too. The Universe responds to the emotions you generate. If you want more money, for instance, think about how it would feel to have financial freedom. Feel that feeling of abundance now, even before the money arrives.

   The more vividly you can feel the emotions that align with your desires, the stronger your vibrational signal becomes, and the closer you get to manifesting your goal.

3. **Visualize the Outcome**: Visualization is a powerful tool in the Vibrational Match System. By visualizing your desires in as much detail as possible, you create a mental picture that your energy can attune to. When you visualize your goals regularly, you reinforce the vibration of that desired outcome.

4. **Believe You Deserve It**: Limiting beliefs and self-doubt are some of the biggest obstacles to matching your vibration with your desires. If you don't believe you are worthy of your desires or if you doubt that they're possible, you'll emit a low vibration that repels the things you want. On the other hand, believing in your worth and deservingness strengthens your vibrational match.

The Vibrational Match System operates on the understanding that the Universe only responds to the energy you put out. This means that if you're not aligned with your desires, you'll have a hard time attracting them.

Think of it like trying to tune into a radio station. If you're tuned to 90.7 FM, you'll hear music from that station. But if you're tuned to 103.5 FM, you won't hear the same music. Similarly, if your vibration is not in sync with the frequency of your desires, you won't attract them. The more aligned your energy is with what you want, the more likely you are to see it manifest in your reality.

This also explains why some people seem to manifest their desires quickly while others struggle. The people who manifest quickly are usually already in alignment with their desires—whether consciously or unconsciously. They are vibrating at the same frequency as their goals. Those who struggle often have mental blocks or limiting beliefs that prevent them from aligning with their desires, which means their vibration is out of sync.

*Practical Ways to Align Your
Vibration with Your Desires*

Now that you understand how the Vibrational Match System works, let's explore practical steps to ensure you're aligned with what you want to manifest.

1. Practice Gratitude: Gratitude is one of the most powerful ways to raise your vibration. When you focus on the positive aspects of your life, you attract more of the same. Spend a few minutes each day writing down what you're grateful for, whether it's your health, your family, your job, or even small things like a cup of coffee. The more gratitude you express, the higher your vibration will be, and the closer you'll get to your desires.

2. Affirmations and Positive Self-Talk: Affirmations are powerful tools for shifting your energy. By repeating positive statements, you reprogram your subconscious mind to believe

in the possibility of your desires. For example, "I am worthy of abundance," or "I attract opportunities that align with my goals." These statements help you shift your mindset to match the vibration of abundance and success.

3. Take Inspired Action: Aligning your vibration also requires you to act in ways that are in harmony with your goals. Look for opportunities that feel good and move you closer to what you want. If you're visualizing a promotion at work, take actions that reflect readiness for that role—whether it's learning new skills, taking on extra responsibility, or making connections with the right people.

4. Cultivate Joy: When you do things that make you feel good, your vibration automatically rises. Make time for activities that bring you joy, whether it's spending time with loved ones, pursuing hobbies, or simply relaxing. The more you focus on things that bring you happiness, the more your energy will be aligned with abundance and success.

5. Release Resistance: Resistance is one of the biggest blocks to manifestation. When you feel anxious, fearful, or desperate, you're sending out a low-frequency vibration that can block your desires. Let go of the need to control everything. Trust that your desires are on their way and release any fear or doubt that they won't come to you.

The Vibrational Match System is one of the most powerful concepts in the manifestation process. It's about aligning your thoughts, feelings, beliefs, and actions with the energy of what you want to manifest. When you tune into the right frequency, you become a magnet for the experiences, people, and opportunities that will help you create your ideal life.

By understanding how to align with your desires and raise your vibration, you can begin to attract everything you've ever dreamed of. Remember, the Universe is always responding to the energy you put out. So, focus on being a vibrational match for your goals, and watch the magic unfold.

How Resistance Blocks Attraction

What Is Resistance?

Resistance, in the context of manifestation, refers to the internal energy or emotions that oppose your desires. It's when you unknowingly or consciously block the natural flow of abundance, success, or love that the Universe is trying to send your way.

Imagine you're trying to drive a car forward, but you're simultaneously pressing the brakes. No matter how much gas you give it, the car won't move forward as smoothly. Resistance is like pressing the brakes on your manifestations.

But how does this work? And why do we resist what we want most?

Why Do We Resist Our Desires?

Resistance often comes from fear, doubt, or a lack of trust in the manifestation process. It's deeply rooted in our subconscious mind, which tends to play a major role in how we create our reality.

Here are some common causes of resistance:

1. Fear of Change: Even when we desire something better—whether it's more money, a loving relationship, or a fulfilling

career—the fear of change can hold us back. This fear is often linked to our comfort zones. Change, even positive change, can feel uncertain, and our subconscious mind tends to resist the unknown.

2. Fear of Failure or Rejection: Many people fear they won't succeed, so they hold back from fully embracing their desires. This fear of failure or rejection often stems from past experiences where things didn't go as planned. These past disappointments can create a belief that they will fail again, causing a subconscious block to their desires.

3. Limiting Beliefs: Our beliefs about ourselves and the world around us shape the way we manifest. If we believe, deep down, that we're not worthy of success or that the Universe doesn't have enough to offer, this belief will block us from receiving what we desire. These limiting beliefs create resistance because they don't match the frequency of abundance, love, or success we want to attract.

4. Doubt and Uncertainty: When you're unsure whether manifestation works or doubt that you deserve your desires, you create energetic friction. Doubt is a powerful resistance force—it's like sending mixed signals to the Universe. On one hand, you say you want something, but on the other, you doubt it's possible, which creates a conflicting vibration.

5. Attachment to Outcomes: Attachment to a specific outcome can also create resistance. When you hold on tightly to a specific idea of how your desires should show up, you create rigidity in your energy. This restricts the flow of possibilities and can block manifestations from arriving in unexpected, yet perfectly aligned, ways.

Resistance essentially acts as a vibrational mismatch between what you want and the energy you're putting out into the Universe. Since the Law of Attraction operates on the principle that like attracts like, the energy you send out must be in alignment with your desires.

Let's explore how resistance disrupts this alignment:

1. Lower Vibrational Frequency

Resistance often brings negative emotions such as frustration, anxiety, doubt, or fear. These emotions operate at a lower frequency compared to the higher vibrations of joy, gratitude, love, and abundance. When you're experiencing negative emotions or stuck in a state of resistance, you're not emitting the high-frequency energy needed to attract what you desire.

The Universe can only bring you experiences that match your vibration. If you're in a state of resistance, you're sending out conflicting signals. You may desire wealth, but if you're anxious or afraid of not having enough, the Universe can only match you with more fear, scarcity, and lack. It's like trying to tune into a station on the radio but constantly turning the dial to the wrong frequency.

2. Sending Mixed Signals

When you resist something, it means that on one level, you want it, but on another level, you're repelling it. Resistance is a signal of internal conflict. For example, you may want a new job, but you fear that you're not qualified enough or won't find a job that truly satisfies you. Your desire for a fulfilling career is at odds with your belief that it's impossible or that you'll fail. This internal contradiction sends mixed signals to the Universe, creating resistance and slowing down manifestation.

3. Holding onto Negative Expectations

Often, resistance stems from the belief that your desires are too difficult to attain or that things won't work out. When you carry negative expectations, you're essentially blocking the very thing you want to manifest. This happens because you're creating an energetic barrier with your thoughts and emotions. When you expect failure, that's exactly what the Universe will mirror back to you.

4. Creating Desperation and Lack

Another way resistance blocks attraction is through attachment. When you become desperate or overly fixated on a specific outcome, you are focusing on what you don't have, rather than what you desire. This desperation emits the energy of lack and neediness, which is exactly what you don't want to attract. The Universe responds to feelings of abundance, not lack. When you come from a place of already having, you align yourself with the energy of having more. But when you're focused on not having enough, you block the flow.

The good news is that resistance can be overcome. When you release resistance, you open up to the natural flow of abundance and allow the Universe to deliver what you truly desire. Here are practical steps to release resistance and allow the Law of Attraction to work more effectively for you:

1. Shift Your Focus to Gratitude

Gratitude is one of the highest vibrational states you can enter. When you focus on what you're grateful for, you naturally raise your vibration and release feelings of lack or resistance. By practicing gratitude daily, you begin to align yourself with the energy of abundance.

2. Let Go of the Need for Control

Often, resistance comes from trying to control how and when your desires show up. The key to releasing resistance is to practice detachment. Trust that the Universe knows the best way to deliver your desires, even if it doesn't look the way you expect. Let go of your attachment to a specific outcome, and allow the Universe to work its magic.

3. Identify and Challenge Limiting Beliefs

Take time to uncover any limiting beliefs that may be blocking your manifestations. Ask yourself: "What beliefs do I hold about money, success, or love that might be holding me back?" Once you've identified these beliefs, work to shift them. Use affirmations, visualization, or journaling to reprogram your subconscious mind and align your beliefs with your desires.

4. Practice Mindfulness and Self-Awareness

Sometimes, resistance is subtle and unconscious. Becoming aware of your thoughts, feelings, and actions can help you identify when you're slipping into a state of resistance. Mindfulness practices, such as meditation, can help you become more present and recognize when negative thoughts or emotions arise. Once you're aware, you can consciously choose to shift your focus to something more positive and empowering.

5. Cultivate Patience and Trust

Trust that your desires are on their way to you, even if they haven't manifested yet. Patience is key in the manifestation process. Resist the urge to force things or get frustrated. Trust that the Universe is working behind the scenes to bring your desires to you in perfect timing.

Resistance blocks the flow of your desires because it creates a vibrational mismatch. Whether it's fear, doubt, limiting beliefs, or attachment to specific outcomes, resistance sends out negative energy that repels your goals. However, by becoming aware of your resistance and learning to release it, you open the doors for abundance, success, and love to flow into your life.

By practicing gratitude, letting go of control, and addressing limiting beliefs, you can remove the internal blocks that prevent you from attracting what you desire. Remember, manifestation is a process of alignment. When you stop resisting, you allow the Universe to bring you the experiences that match your highest vibration.

Chapter 5

Speak It Into Existence – The Power of Incantations

Incantations vs. Affirmations: What's the Difference and Why It Matters

At first glance, incantations and affirmations might seem like the same thing—they both involve repeating positive statements to reprogram your mindset. But there's a crucial difference in how they're practiced, how they're felt, and ultimately, how effective they are.

Affirmations are often quiet, passive statements like "I am confident," "I am successful," or "Money flows to me." They're usually repeated silently or softly, sometimes written down or spoken in front of a mirror. Affirmations work best when they're consistent and emotionally believable, but for many people, they can feel hollow if the underlying belief hasn't caught up yet. If you're saying "I am abundant" while secretly stressing about your bank balance, the affirmation may clash with your current emotional state, making it hard for the subconscious mind to accept it as truth.

Incantations, on the other hand, add a crucial missing ingredient: emotion and embodiment. They're designed to be said out loud, with power, and often while moving your body or changing your physical state. Think: raised voice, energized tone, strong posture, eye contact with yourself in the mirror—or even pacing, jumping, or clapping as you speak. It's about *feeling* the truth of what you're saying, not just stating it.

When you declare something like:

"I am unstoppable. I am focused. I create results!"

With conviction, loud and proud, while moving your body and breathing deeply, your nervous system begins to align with that statement. You're not just *saying* the words—you're experiencing them in your body. That experience builds emotional momentum, which is exactly what impresses the subconscious mind.

Tony Robbins, who popularized the concept of incantations, often says that "emotion is created by motion." By moving your body and charging your words with energy, you anchor the new belief more powerfully. Your subconscious isn't just hearing a new thought—it's feeling it, which makes it easier to accept and act on.

Here's a simple example:

- Affirmation: "I am worthy of love."
- Incantation (spoken with emotion, movement, and repetition):
- "I AM love. I radiate love. I attract deep, beautiful connections effortlessly—because I AM worthy!"

See the difference?

The first feels like a statement. The second feels like a command. A new energetic instruction is being programmed into your body and mind.

The truth is, you can repeat affirmations for months and not see much change if you're doing it mechanically. But say an incantation every day for 30 days, with energy, emotion, and belief—even if you have to fake it at first—and you'll start noticing shifts. In how you feel. How you carry yourself. And in the outcomes you begin attracting.

This matters because manifestation isn't just mental—it's energetic. You're not just thinking your life into being. You're speaking it. Feeling it. Embodying it. Incantations give you a way to *live into* your next-level self before the evidence shows up—and that's exactly what speeds up the manifestation process.

Rewiring Your Subconscious Through Repetition and Emotion

Your subconscious mind is the silent architect of your life. It governs your habits, reactions, self-worth, and what you unconsciously believe is possible for you. The challenge is: that it doesn't update itself just because you want a new life. It only rewires through consistent repetition and, more importantly, emotion.

Let's break that down.

Your subconscious mind doesn't understand logic in the way your conscious mind does. It responds best to patterns—

repeated messages backed by feeling. Think about it: most of your core beliefs were formed during your early years not because someone explained them rationally, but because they were experienced emotionally and repeated often. If you were told repeatedly as a child that you were "too loud" or "not smart enough," you didn't just hear those words—you felt the sting, the rejection, the shame. Over time, that emotional repetition embedded the belief into your subconscious as truth.

Now, here's the good news: you can rewire those beliefs. But it won't happen by telling yourself a new story once or twice. It takes intention, energy, and consistency. That's where incantations become such a powerful tool. When practiced with emotion, incantations act as a counter-programming force—you're installing a new belief system by overriding the old one, just like updating outdated software.

Here's why repetition works so well:

- The subconscious mind learns through rehearsal. Just like practicing an instrument, repeating a new belief or statement carves a new neural pathway in the brain.
- The more often you fire those pathways, the stronger they become. What once felt like a stretch ("I am abundant") starts to feel natural, automatic, even self-evident.

But repetition alone is not enough.

Emotion is the glue. It's what tells your subconscious, *"Hey, this is important—pay attention!"* If repetition is the hammer, emotion is the force behind the swing. Without it, you're tapping gently. With it, you're creating lasting change.

That's why saying your incantations in a flat, monotone voice or while scrolling your phone isn't going to move the needle. You need to bring the feeling behind the words. Even if it feels silly or unnatural at first, the goal is to make your body believe it's already true. That's when the subconscious starts responding.

Let's say your incantation is:

"I am a magnet for wealth and opportunities. Abundance flows to me from all directions."

Now imagine saying that out loud, arms open, shoulders back, breathing deeply, with a smile on your face. Do it every morning. After a few days, something will shift. Not just in your mood, but in how you see yourself—and how you start acting. Your energy, your posture, and the way you carry yourself begins to match that statement. And your reality starts to respond.

This is the foundation of embodiment. You're not waiting for external proof before you believe something—you're choosing to believe it *now* and letting your internal belief system lead the way. That's the magnetizing effect that fuels manifestation. When your inner state shifts, your outer life follows.

Another powerful technique is to pair your incantations with a trigger—a movement, gesture, or time of day that anchors the habit. For example, you might:

- Say your incantations out loud while walking in nature.
- Repeat them while doing jumping jacks to activate energy.
- Speak them in the mirror first thing in the morning, locking eyes with yourself.

These rituals create muscle memory for your new belief system.

And if you really want to supercharge it, combine incantations with visualization. Speak your incantation while picturing yourself living the reality it describes. Engage all your senses. What are you wearing? Who's with you? How does it feel in your body? The more vivid the emotional experience, the deeper the subconscious imprint.

In time, this repetition + emotion formula transforms how you think, how you show up, and what you attract. You begin to *expect* success, love, and abundance—not as wishful thinking, but as a natural extension of who you are becoming.

Creating Your Personal Incantations: A Step-by-Step Practice

Incantations are most powerful when they're personal—crafted by *you*, for *you*. While it's helpful to borrow powerful phrases or examples from others, the incantations that truly change your inner wiring are the ones that speak directly to your desires, your growth, and your identity shift.

Here's a simple, effective step-by-step method to create your own incantations and start using them to reprogram your mind and energy:

Step 1: Identify the Old Story You Want to Rewrite

Start by getting honest about the core belief or pattern you want to transform. What's a recurring thought, fear, or limitation that keeps showing up in your life?

Examples:

- "I never have enough money."
- "I always mess things up."
- "I'm not good enough."
- "Love never lasts for me."

Write it down. Then, write a few ways that belief has impacted your life so far. This helps you bring subconscious patterns into conscious awareness—and that's the first step to changing them.

Step 2: Flip the Script Into Empowering Truths

Now take that old belief and write the opposite, but in a way that feels *empowering, believable*, and emotionally charged.

Example:

Old belief: "I'm not good enough."

New incantation:

"I am more than enough. I was born worthy. I am proud of who I am becoming."

Don't just negate the old thought—replace it with a bold new identity statement. Use words that light you up, words that feel strong and expansive. Think about how your future self would speak about this area of life.

Pro tip: Start your incantations with phrases like:

- "I am…"
- "I always…"

- "I attract…"
- "I choose…"
- "I create…"

Step 3: Add Emotion and Movement

Once you've got your new incantation, practice saying it out loud—not in a whisper, but with presence. Feel it in your chest, your voice, your posture. Say it like you mean it.

Want to amplify the effect?

- Stand tall, shoulders back, and say it in front of a mirror.
- Pace or move your body as you speak.
- Breathe deeply and intentionally as you repeat the phrase.
- Repeat it 10–20 times each session for maximum impact.

The goal is to link the words with emotion and energy, creating a whole-body experience.

Step 4: Make It a Ritual

Repetition is key. You're not trying this out—you're installing it.

Set a daily ritual:

- Mornings: Say your incantations as soon as you wake up.
- Evenings: Repeat them before bed to impress your subconscious while you sleep.
- Transitions: Use incantations to reset your energy throughout the day (before a meeting, during a walk, etc.).

You can even record yourself saying them and listen back during quiet moments or when you need a boost.

Step 5: Adjust and Evolve

As you grow, your incantations will evolve too. What feels bold and expansive now might feel natural and obvious in a few months—that's a good sign! Update your phrases to reflect your next level of expansion.

Also, if you ever feel resistant to saying an incantation, explore why. Does it feel fake? Too far from your current reality? That's a signal to either scale the wording to something your nervous system can accept or do the deeper work around worthiness and belief.

Examples of Personal Incantations

Here are a few to inspire you:

- "I am magnetic to abundance in every form. Opportunities chase me down."
- "I am calm, capable, and clear under pressure."
- "I am a powerful creator. My thoughts shape my reality."
- "I love who I am, and I attract love that reflects that."

The most important part? Feel it. Embody it. Even if it feels awkward at first, keep going. The more you practice, the more natural it becomes—and eventually, the more *true* it feels. That's when the shift happens. That's when you start showing up differently… and the world responds in kind.

Turn to the back of the book to create your own Incantation.

Chapter 6

Visualization, Affirmations, and Scripting

How to Visualize Properly (Most People Get It Wrong)

Let's clear this up right away: visualization is not about closing your eyes and hoping for a miracle. It's not about seeing the thing you want and crossing your fingers. Visualization is a mental training technique rooted in neuroscience and psychology—and most people misuse it by focusing on outcomes, not experiences. The difference is subtle but transformational.

You see, the goal of visualization isn't just to "see the thing." It's to feel yourself living it. And that's where most people get stuck. They visualize from a distance, like watching a movie on a screen. But your brain responds best when you're *in* the movie, not just watching it.

So, let's break this down. Here's how to visualize properly—so your subconscious believes the story you're telling.

1. Make It a "First-Person Experience"

You want your mind to register your visualizations as something you're living now, not something you're just observing. So instead of picturing yourself like a character in a film, step into the scene. Visualize through your own eyes.

If you want to manifest a new home, don't picture yourself standing across the street admiring the house. Walk through the front door. Hear your footsteps echo. Smell the fresh paint or the scent of your favorite candle. Touch the doorknob, sit on the sofa, look out the window—*as if you're already there.* This is immersive, first-person visualization.

When you do it this way, you trick your subconscious into thinking, "This is real." That's what you want. The subconscious governs your habits, your identity, and your sense of safety. And it only accepts change when it feels familiar and emotionally congruent.

2. Anchor the Visualization in Emotion

Emotion is what stamps the experience into your subconscious. This is where most visualizations fall flat. People think the image is enough, but it's actually the feeling that transmits the frequency.

If you're visualizing financial freedom, don't just picture numbers in your bank account. Ask yourself: *What does freedom feel like?* Is it peace? Relief? Confidence? Pride? Gratitude?

Let those feelings rise in your body as you visualize. Take a breath and allow the sensation to move through you. Smile. Cry. Put your hand on your heart. Whatever helps you embody the emotional state. The more real it feels the more powerful the imprint.

3. Add Multi-Sensory Details

You don't need to be a visual thinker to visualize. In fact, some people "see" more with sound, touch, or inner knowing. That's all valid.

Try asking yourself:

- What am I seeing?
- What can I hear?
- What do I smell?
- What can I feel on my skin?
- What emotions are coming up?

The more senses you involve, the more your brain believes it's happening. Remember: the mind loves clarity and familiarity. The vaguer the scene, the less impact it has.

4. Be Consistent, Not Sporadic

You don't brush your teeth once and expect perfect dental health, right? Visualization is the same. It's not about doing it once with fireworks—it's about doing it *regularly* and *intentionally*.

Even 5–10 minutes a day can create massive shifts if you do it consistently. Morning is powerful because your brain is in a theta state—open and receptive. Before bed is another great time, as you're winding down and influencing your subconscious before sleep.

Set a routine. Tie it to something you already do—after your coffee, before your workout, right before sleep. Make it non-negotiable. Like brushing your inner world clean.

5. Don't Visualize the "How"—Visualize the "Feeling of Having"

This one is key: Don't try to visualize every step of how it will happen. That's control, not creation. The universe fills in the path. Your job is to hold the vision and the emotion of the end result.

Imagine already living the life you desire. Skip the awkward middle. See yourself already there—and feel what it's like. That's the frequency you need to match.

For example, if you want to manifest love, don't visualize dating apps' first dates or texts. Go straight to the moment: you're laughing together at dinner, curled up watching a movie, holding hands on a walk. The *end feeling*. That's what sends the clearest signal.

6. End with Gratitude

After each visualization session, close with gratitude. Not just "thank you in advance"—but thank you as if it already happened. Gratitude is the emotional signature of receiving. It creates a loop that tells your subconscious, "This is mine. I trust it's done."

Say it out loud if you can. Smile. Let it settle in your body.

"I'm so grateful this is now my life."

"Thank you for guiding me here."

"Thank you, thank you, thank you."

Visualization, when done right, becomes a tool to *train your nervous system to expect your desires.* It rewires your default state. Over time, you'll find your thoughts, habits, and decisions start aligning naturally with your vision—because you've already been there, over and over again.

This isn't fluff. This is how Olympic athletes prepare. It's how entrepreneurs prime for success. It's how you move from "I wish" to "This is mine."

Ready to build that inner movie every day?

Writing to Your Future Self: A Manifestation Tool That Builds Identity and Trust

There's something powerful about putting pen to paper and speaking directly to the version of you who already *has* what you're working toward. When you write to your future self, you're doing more than imagining a better life—you're anchoring it. You're bridging the gap between "one day" and *this is happening.*

This isn't about fantasy or fiction. It's about aligning your subconscious with the version of you that already knows the path, already overcome the hurdles, and is living the life you dream about today.

Why Writing to Your Future Self Works

Most of us are programmed to think from the past: old stories, inherited beliefs, and childhood wounds. When you write to your future self, you flip that script. You begin to think from the future, which is the fastest way to align with it.

It works on several levels:

- Psychologically, it primes your brain to expect success and act accordingly.
- Emotionally, it softens resistance by creating a sense of inevitability.
- Energetically, it signals to the universe that you're already becoming the version of yourself who can hold what you're asking for.

This is an identity-level manifestation—not just "wanting" but *being*.

How to Write to Your Future Self (Step-by-Step)

You can do this as a one-time letter, a weekly ritual, or even a daily journaling practice. What matters is consistency, clarity, and emotional truth.

Here's how to get started:

Step 1: Choose the Timeline

Ask yourself: *How far ahead do I want to write from?*

6 months? One year? Three years?

Pick a time frame that feels both exciting and believable. Long enough to create change, but close enough that you can emotionally connect to it.

Step 2: Get Specific About the Version of You

Before you start writing, take 2–3 minutes to close your eyes and visualize this version of you. Where are you living? What do your days look like? How do you feel when you wake up? Who's in your life? What kind of work are you doing?

Let the images and emotions come up, and then write from that energy. This helps activate the subconscious, which doesn't respond to logic—it responds to clarity and feeling.

Step 3: Start the Letter as If You're Already There

Write in the present tense. No "I hope" or "I want." Step into the shoes of the *you who's already arrived.*

Here's an example:

Dear Me,

Wow. What a ride it's been. I'm sitting in my new kitchen right now, the sun pouring through the windows, listening to my favorite playlist, and sipping my morning smoothie. Life feels so grounded and joyful now. I'm proud of how I stayed the course, even when it was hard.

Describe the world around you, how you feel, and what you've overcome. Thank your current self for being brave, trusting, and patient. Encourage them. Tell them the things *you* need to hear today but from the voice of you who's made it.

Step 4: Make Space for the Emotion

Don't just list what happened. Let yourself *feel* it. What does confidence feel like in your body? What does financial peace feel like in your chest? What kind of joy shows up when you're in alignment?

This is where the transformation happens. The more you let yourself *feel* the letter, the more the subconscious accepts it as a new normal.

Step 5: Reread Often

This isn't a letter to tuck away and forget. Come back to it. Especially on hard days. Read it out loud. Add to it. Let it evolve. Let it remind you that your future self is already cheering you on—and your job is simply to show up for them now.

Reading it daily or weekly reprograms your identity. Over time, you'll notice that your choices, habits, and even language start to shift to align with the future you've written.

Optional Twist: Reverse the Letter

You can also try writing as your future self to your present self. Flip the roles. Let the wiser, calmer, more fulfilled version of you speak encouragement, clarity, or reassurance over where you are now.

Example:

Hey you,

I know this part feels uncertain, but I promise—it's all unfolding. The work you're doing now matters. Every morning you showed up, even when you weren't sure it was working, moved the needle. I'm proud of you. Keep going. You're almost here.

Sometimes, what we need isn't new information—it's the reminder that we're already on the path. A letter like this can become your personal anchor.

Writing to your future self is one of the simplest and most powerful manifestation tools you can use. It collapses time. It shifts your state. It gives your subconscious new instructions to follow—and new evidence to expect.

Affirmations That Actually Work (Science-Backed)

Affirmations have become a mainstream tool in the manifestation community. However, not all affirmations are created equal. Many people try repeating positive statements, but see little to no results. Why? Because affirmations work only when they are aligned with neuroscience and the way the brain processes information. Simply repeating "I am wealthy" without any emotional connection or belief will likely have little effect.

To make affirmations truly work, we need to understand how they interact with our subconscious mind—and how we can scientifically make them more effective.

1. The Neuroscience of Affirmations: Rewiring the Brain

Your brain operates on neural pathways—clusters of neurons that fire together, creating patterns of thought and behavior. These pathways are formed by your repeated thoughts and experiences. The more often you think a certain thought, the stronger that pathway becomes.

When you use affirmations, you're essentially creating new neural pathways. By repeatedly speaking positive statements, you strengthen the brain's ability to accept new beliefs and behaviors. The challenge is that if your affirmation doesn't resonate with your current reality, your subconscious mind will resist it. This can lead to cognitive dissonance, where your mind rejects the affirmation as "not true."

Here's the science-backed solution: Rather than using generic, over-the-top affirmations like "I am a millionaire," choose affirmations that are realistic and closely aligned with your current beliefs. For instance, affirmations like "I am becoming more confident every day" or "I am open to new opportunities for financial growth" feel more achievable to the brain and are more likely to stick.

2. The Power of "I Am" Statements

"I am" statements are particularly effective in affirmations because they reinforce identity. According to research in psychology, the self-concept is central to your behavior and motivation. When you affirm an identity, you're not just stating a goal; you're embedding that goal into your very sense of who you are.

A study by Dr. David Creswell at Carnegie Mellon University found that affirmations can help reduce stress by reinforcing positive aspects of self-identity. The "I am" affirmations help to rewire your brain's perception of who you are, thus aligning your actions with this new identity.

For example, when you say, "I am confident," your brain begins to adjust your perceptions, actions, and even physiology (like posture or speech patterns) to reflect that new identity. Over time, you begin to act and think like a confident person.

3. Emotion: The Key to Effective Affirmations

If you're not feeling the affirmation, it's unlikely to have any long-term effect. Science tells us that emotion is the key to creating change in the brain. The amygdala, which processes emotions, is activated when we have strong emotional responses to events. This makes emotional experiences much easier for the brain to remember and internalize.

When you pair affirmations with genuine feelings—whether it's excitement, gratitude, or relief—you enhance their power. For example, if you're affirming financial abundance, really feel the excitement of receiving that money. Imagine what you would do with it. How would you spend it? How would it feel in your hands? The more emotion you can attach to the affirmation, the more likely it is that the affirmation will impact your brain and actions.

4. The Power of Repetition

You've probably heard that "practice makes perfect," and there's a scientific reason for that. Repetition helps the brain strengthen neural connections, making your affirmations more effective over time. This is rooted in the principle of neuroplasticity, which is the brain's ability to rewire itself throughout life. The more you repeat an affirmation, the more your brain comes to believe it.

However, it's essential to note that repetition must be consistent and intentional. Instead of saying your affirmation mindlessly, take a few moments to focus on it. Feel it deeply. Allow it to shift your emotional state. Over time, your brain will begin to incorporate this new belief as part of your identity.

5. Combine Affirmations with Action

Affirmations alone will not manifest your desires if you don't take action. However, they can motivate you to take the right steps. Neuroscientific studies have shown that positive affirmations can trigger actions in line with your desired goals.

For instance, a study published in *Psychological Science* by Dr. Michael Inzlicht and his team found that participants who repeated affirmations related to their goals were more likely to take positive actions and make better decisions. This is because affirmations help reinforce your focus and motivation. When you affirm, "I am a successful entrepreneur," your brain will push you to seek out opportunities, stay resilient through challenges, and take the necessary actions to build your business.

To truly make affirmations work, the science backs up a few simple guidelines:

- Choose affirmations that align with your current beliefs to avoid cognitive dissonance.
- Use "I am" statements to reinforce your sense of self.
- Pair your affirmations with strong emotions to increase their effectiveness.
- Repeat them regularly, but consciously. Repetition is key, but emotional connection is what seals the deal.
- Take inspired action. Affirmations will guide you, but you still have to act on the opportunities they bring.

When used intentionally and with the right mindset, affirmations can become one of the most powerful tools in your manifestation toolkit. And now, you know the science behind it.

Chapter 7

Inspired Action vs. Forced Hustle

What Is "Inspired" Action?

In the world of manifestation, we often hear that "action" is a key ingredient to bringing our desires into reality. But what kind of action are we talking about? It's not about just taking any random action or forcing yourself into doing something that feels like a grind. It's about taking inspired action—an action that is fueled by intuition, alignment, and a deep sense of knowing that you're on the right path.

Let's break down what inspired action really is and how you can tap into it to manifest your dreams with ease.

The Difference Between Action and Inspired Action

At its core, action is any behavior you take toward achieving a goal. It could be anything from writing an email to launching a product or making a phone call. On the surface, action is necessary, and without it, nothing will move forward. However, most people make the mistake of relying solely on "willpower" or a sense of urgency to push through their goals.

This type of action is often forceful, disconnected from inner guidance, and sometimes even exhausting.

Inspired action, on the other hand, is the opposite. It's a subtle, yet powerful, form of action that comes from a place of deep inspiration, alignment, and intuition. Inspired action is effortless. It doesn't feel like a struggle, and often, it feels like you're being guided or "led" toward the next step.

It's that moment when something clicks inside you, and you just *know* what to do, when to do it, and why it's the right thing to do. Inspired action feels natural—like you're not forcing it but rather *flowing with it*.

How to Recognize Inspired Action

Not every action is inspired, and not every impulse you feel is guidance. So how can you tell when an action is truly inspired?

1. It Feels Aligned with Your Values and Vision

Inspired action comes from within—it resonates with your core values and goals. It doesn't feel like a chore or something you *should* do because someone else expects it. It aligns with who you are and the version of yourself you are becoming.

For example, if you've always dreamed of starting a business that helps people, and one day you feel a sudden urge to email a potential partner for a collaboration, that could be inspired action. It fits your long-term vision, and when you think about it, it feels right.

2. It Feels Energizing Rather Than Draining

Inspired action gives you energy. It doesn't deplete you. Even if the task is challenging, there's a deep satisfaction and excitement behind it. You might feel nervous or excited, but you don't feel drained.

On the flip side, uninspired action may feel draining, like you're pushing a boulder uphill. It can also come with feelings of resentment or impatience. If the action feels like a heavy burden, it may be your intuition telling you to pause and reevaluate.

3. It Often Feels Spontaneous

One of the key qualities of inspired action is that it tends to come spontaneously. It's not premeditated or forced. You don't have to sit down and meticulously plan it out (though planning has its time and place). Instead, inspired action feels like an intuitive nudge that just pops into your mind.

For example, while meditating, you might get an idea to reach out to someone you haven't spoken to in a while, and this connection leads to a breakthrough. That is inspired action in motion.

4. It Feels Like a Step Toward Your Goal, Not Away From It

When you take inspired action, even if it feels small or insignificant in the moment, it's still a step toward your goal. It's a progression, a flow, rather than a stagnant, disconnected action.

If you're looking to manifest abundance, an inspired action could be sending an email to an old client, even though it feels unexpected. That connection might lead to an opportunity you hadn't foreseen, but it aligns with the abundance you desire. It may not be the "big step" you were envisioning, but it is a vital part of the process.

Manifestation isn't just about thinking positively and waiting for things to happen. Action is required, but not just any action—inspired action.

When you take action from a place of alignment and intuition, you begin to co-create with the universe. You are actively participating in your own manifestation, but in a way that doesn't feel like a forced effort.

Here's why it works:

1. It Trusts the Process

Inspired action is about trusting that the universe is guiding you. It's not about controlling every single step. It's about showing up and being ready when the opportunities arise.

The more you take inspired action, the more you build faith in the process of manifestation. You start to trust that you are always in the right place at the right time. You can rest in knowing that every step, no matter how small, is part of a greater plan.

2. It Moves You Beyond Limiting Beliefs

When you act from inspiration, you break free from the limitations of your mind. In contrast to forceful action, which is often riddled with fear and doubt, inspired action comes from a space of confidence and clarity.

For instance, if you're manifesting a successful business but have a subconscious belief that you're not "good enough" to be a leader, you might hesitate to take bold action. But inspired action bypasses that fear. It doesn't feel like you're pushing yourself; instead, it's more like you're being pulled by your own desire, higher purpose, and inner knowing.

How to Tap into Inspired Action

Now that you understand the power of inspired action, how can you start tapping into it more regularly?

- **Stay Grounded in Your Vision:** The clearer your vision, the easier it is to recognize what is aligned with it. Regularly check in with your goals and make sure your actions reflect your true desires.
- **Trust Your Intuition:** Listen to your inner guidance. Trust that gut feeling. Inspired action often feels like a "knowing," and it's usually accompanied by a sense of excitement or calm assurance.
- **Let Go of Control:** Don't micromanage the manifestation process. Instead, take inspired steps when they come to you, without forcing yourself into unnecessary action.
- **Embrace the Flow:** Inspired action is about flowing with life, not pushing against it. Trust that you are being guided to the right place at the right time.

Inspired action is the heart of manifestation. It's where the magic happens. It's where your dreams shift from the abstract to the tangible. And while it may not always look the way you imagined, it's always in perfect alignment with your soul's path.

So the next time you feel that little nudge or impulse to take a step toward your goal, trust it. Embrace it. It's your invitation to move closer to what you've been asking for. Keep taking inspired action, and watch your manifestations unfold effortlessly.

Signs from the Universe and Synchronicity

One of the most exciting and awe-inspiring parts of the manifestation journey is recognizing that the universe is always communicating with you. Whether it's through the appearance of a specific number, a random encounter, or a sudden flash of insight, the universe speaks to you in countless ways. This is where the concept of synchronicity comes in.

Synchronicity is the term coined by renowned psychologist Carl Jung to describe the meaningful coincidences that seem to happen just when you need them most. They're not random at all, but signs that you're in alignment with your desires. Understanding and interpreting these signs can not only help you stay on track but also enhance your manifestation process.

What Are Signs from the Universe?

Signs from the universe are subtle clues or messages that appear in your life, seemingly at random but are deeply connected to your thoughts, desires, and intentions. They may come in the form of:

- Repeating numbers (like 11:11, 333, 444, etc.)
- Unexpected opportunities or encounters that seem "too perfect" to be coincidental
- Visions, dreams, or sudden insights that feel significant

- Animals, songs, or symbols that seem to appear in moments when you're thinking about something important

While some people might dismiss these as coincidences, those who are tuned into the universe's subtle language recognize them as a form of divine guidance. These signs aren't just random; they are the universe's way of showing you that you're on the right path, nudging you toward a decision, or reassuring you that your desires are being heard.

The Role of Synchronicity in Manifestation

Synchronicity is the phenomenon where two seemingly unrelated events occur at the same time, yet they hold deep, meaningful significance to you. When you're manifesting something, you might start noticing that certain events, people, or opportunities appear just when you need them—often in unexpected ways.

For instance, let's say you've been visualizing a new job opportunity, and out of the blue, a friend tells you about an opening at a company that's been on your mind. Or, perhaps you see a car with a license plate that has the number of your dream home's street on it, just when you were thinking about how to make the purchase possible. These are examples of synchronicities that serve as confirmation that your thoughts are in alignment with your desires.

It's important to understand that synchronicity isn't about forcing things to happen. It's about being open and receptive to the clues that show up naturally. The universe works in mysterious ways, and often, it's through synchronicity that your manifestations take shape.

How to Recognize and Interpret Signs

The key to recognizing signs and synchronicity is awareness. The more tuned in you are to the world around you, the more likely you are to notice these seemingly small, but important, occurrences. Here are a few tips for interpreting signs from the universe:

1. Pay Attention to Your Intuition

When you notice a sign or synchronicity, check in with your gut. How does it make you feel? If it feels like a "yes" or sparks excitement, that's often your intuition confirming that it's meaningful. If you feel uneasy or unsure, it may not be the right time or sign.

2. Keep a Journal

Start tracking the signs and synchronicities you encounter. Write down the date, time, and context. Over time, you may begin to notice patterns or recurring themes that help you understand the messages better. For example, if you constantly see the number 1111, it might symbolize a reminder to stay focused on your goals or to align your thoughts with your desires.

3. Trust the Timing

Synchronicity often happens when you're in flow, not when you're forcing things. If you're trying to make something happen by sheer willpower, signs may be more difficult to notice. But when you relax and trust the timing of the universe, that's when everything starts to line up.

4. Be Open to Different Forms

Signs may not always come in the form of something directly related to your desires. For example, if you're manifesting financial abundance, you might receive a sign in the form of a reminder to practice self-care or an invitation to meet a new friend. Every sign, big or small, is part of the larger puzzle.

Trusting the Universe's Timing

Often, we expect signs and synchronicity to appear when we're ready for them, but the universe has its own timeline. Sometimes, the best sign it can give us is a period of waiting or stillness. Trust that everything is unfolding exactly as it should. The universe is always working behind the scenes, setting up events and opportunities that align with your desires—sometimes when you least expect them.

It's also important to remain patient. The universe doesn't always deliver things on our schedule. If you've received signs and synchronicities, but things aren't happening as quickly as you'd like, it's a reminder that the timing is still being orchestrated perfectly.

Recognizing signs from the universe and experiencing synchronicity is one of the most magical aspects of the manifestation process. These experiences are invitations to trust, to stay open, and to know that you are being guided every step of the way. When you embrace these signs with gratitude and faith, you tap into the natural flow of the universe, making it easier to manifest your desires with grace and ease.

The universe is always speaking to you—are you listening?

Trusting the Process Without Obsession

Manifestation is a powerful practice, but it can often feel like a delicate balance between setting your intentions and letting go of control. One of the biggest hurdles people face on their manifestation journey is learning to trust the process without becoming overly fixated on the outcome.

In the world of manifestation, we've all heard the advice to "trust the process" or "let go and let the universe work its magic." But what does that actually mean, and how do you apply it without obsessing over the details? The trick is in finding a balance—trusting that everything is unfolding in its perfect timing, without constantly worrying or trying to control every step.

Let's explore why this balance is crucial and how you can stop obsessing about your desires while still actively participating in the manifestation process.

The Power of Detachment in Manifestation

At first glance, detaching from your desires might seem counterintuitive. After all, how can you manifest something if you're not hyper-focused on it? The truth is, that detachment is not about losing interest or giving up on your dreams. It's about releasing the need for control and trusting that the universe is bringing things to you in the right way and at the right time.

When you detach from the outcome, you stop putting pressure on yourself and the universe to make it happen on your timeline. You stop obsessing over every little detail, every step, and every potential obstacle. Instead, you allow things to unfold naturally, which frees up space for you to receive your manifestations with ease.

Think about a seed you plant in the ground. Once it's planted, you water it, care for it, and trust that it will grow. But you don't dig it up every day to check if it's sprouting. You trust the process, even though you can't see the progress right away. Manifestation is very much the same. Trusting the process means knowing that your desires are germinating beneath the surface, even if you can't see immediate results.

The Dangers of Obsessing Over Your Desires

When you're obsessed with a particular outcome, several things can happen that hinder your manifestation process:

1. You're Sending Mixed Signals

Constantly obsessing over a desire can signal a state of lack to the universe. When you're overly focused on the "how" and "when" of your manifestation, you're essentially telling the universe that you don't trust that your desire will arrive. This creates an energy of desperation rather than expectation, which can slow down or block the process.

Think of it like trying to chase after a butterfly. The more you chase it, the more it eludes you. But when you relax, remain still, and trust that the butterfly will come to you, it often lands right on your shoulder.

2. It Creates Anxiety and Doubt

Obsession tends to generate anxiety. You start questioning every step you take and wondering if you're doing enough to bring your manifestation into reality. You may also doubt whether you're deserving or if the universe is really on your side. This creates resistance, which is one of the biggest blocks to manifestation.

The key is to take action when inspired and trust that the universe will handle the details. Let go of the need to control and instead focus on living your life with joy and purpose. This trust eliminates the anxious energy around your desires, allowing them to come to you in a natural, stress-free way.

3. You Miss Opportunities for Growth

Obsessing over the end result means you're not fully present for the journey. The process of manifestation is as much about personal growth as it is about achieving your desires. There are lessons to be learned, new skills to be developed, and opportunities to grow spiritually and emotionally along the way. When you're too focused on the destination, you miss out on the beauty of the process itself.

How to Trust the Process Without Obsessing

So, how can you learn to trust the process without getting consumed by obsession? Here are a few strategies:

1. Surrender the "How"

One of the first steps to trusting the process is to surrender how your manifestation will unfold. You don't need to know every detail or have all the answers. Once you've set your intention, release the need to figure out how it will happen. Trust that the universe is infinitely creative and will find the best possible way to deliver your desires to you.

2. Focus on the Feeling, Not the Form

Rather than fixating on a specific outcome or form, focus on the feeling that you want to experience. For example, instead of obsessing over the exact details of your dream job, focus on how it will make you feel—fulfilled, passionate, excited, and abundant. This allows you to align with the energy of your desires without getting hung up on the specifics.

3. Cultivate Patience

Patience is a vital part of manifestation. The universe doesn't work on our timeline, and that's okay. Trust that everything is unfolding at the right pace. If you find yourself becoming impatient, use that energy as an opportunity to reflect on how far you've come and the growth you've experienced so far. Trusting the timing of the universe is about understanding that what you want will come when you're truly ready for it.

4. Practice Gratitude

Gratitude is one of the most powerful ways to remain in trust and flow. When you focus on what's already good in your life, you create a sense of abundance, which helps you feel confident that your desires are already on their way. When you express gratitude for what you've received—whether it's small blessings or big breakthroughs—you build trust with the universe and reinforce your belief that everything you want is coming.

5. Enjoy the Present Moment

Living in the present moment helps you stay connected to your life as it is, without constantly looking to the future. When you engage fully in the now, you release the need for external validation or immediate results. You begin to experience joy and contentment right where you are, which attracts more of the same energy into your life

Chapter 8

Manifesting Money and Financial Freedom

Money Beliefs to Rewire Now

One of the most important aspects of manifesting financial abundance is addressing your beliefs about money. Many of us have been conditioned to believe certain things about wealth, success, and financial security that limit our ability to attract prosperity into our lives. These limiting money beliefs, often inherited from our families, society, or personal experiences, can unconsciously block the flow of abundance.

In order to manifest money, it's essential to rewire your mindset and replace these outdated, restrictive beliefs with new, empowering ones. This process requires awareness, commitment, and consistent practice. Let's dive into some common money beliefs you may need to rewire and how to shift them to align with financial abundance.

1. "Money is Hard to Come By"

One of the most pervasive beliefs people have is that money is scarce or difficult to acquire. This belief often stems from childhood experiences or cultural conditioning that money is limited and must be worked for through endless struggle. If you hold this belief, you may find yourself constantly chasing after money, feeling as though it's always just out of reach.

How to Rewire:

Instead of seeing money as scarce, start viewing it as abundant and flowing freely into your life. Recognize that money is a tool for your greater good, and there are infinite opportunities to attract it. You can shift your mindset by affirming, "Money flows to me easily and effortlessly," and reminding yourself that opportunities for abundance are everywhere. Cultivate gratitude for the money you do have, and allow yourself to feel abundant, even in small amounts.

2. "You Have to Work Hard to Make Money"

The idea that you must work yourself to exhaustion to earn money is another belief that many people carry. This belief often ties money to effort and labor, suggesting that without tireless work, you won't be able to achieve financial success. If you believe this, you may feel trapped in a cycle of overwork and burnout, never feeling like you're able to truly enjoy your financial rewards.

How to Rewire:

Recognize that working hard does not necessarily mean working long hours or exhausting yourself. Instead, focus on the value you bring to the world and the creative ways you can serve others. Replace the belief that you must sacrifice your health or well-being with the understanding that you can make money while maintaining balance and joy. Say to yourself, "I can create wealth with ease, flow, and joy," and begin to take inspired actions that feel good rather than forced.

3. "I Don't Deserve Money"

Many people have deep-rooted beliefs that they're not worthy of wealth, often due to feelings of guilt or shame about money. Perhaps you've been told that having a lot of money is selfish or that rich people are greedy or dishonest. These ideas can create subconscious barriers to financial success, even when you have the potential to attract abundance.

How to Rewire:

The key to overcoming this belief is understanding that you are inherently worthy of wealth. Money is not a measure of your value as a person. It is simply an energy exchange for the services and value you provide. To rewire this belief, affirm, "I am deserving of financial abundance," and recognize that the more you have, the more you can share and contribute to others. Take steps to reinforce this belief by treating yourself with the respect and self-love you deserve, regardless of your financial situation.

4. "Rich People are Bad or Unethical"

This belief often stems from societal stereotypes and judgments about wealth. Some people believe that financial success comes only through exploitation or dishonesty, or they may think that rich people are somehow less morally upright than those with less money. If you believe that money is inherently tied to unethical behavior, it will be hard to attract abundance into your life.

How to Rewire:

To overcome this belief, start viewing wealthy individuals who align with your values as positive role models. Recognize that money can be used for good, and many rich people use their wealth to improve the world. You don't have to compromise your ethics to become wealthy. In fact, the more you align with integrity and purpose, the more you will attract abundance. Affirm, "Money can be used for good, and I choose to use my wealth to serve and help others."

5. "There's Not Enough Money to Go Around"

This belief stems from a scarcity mindset that tells you that wealth is limited. If you believe there is only a finite amount of money, you may feel as though you must compete with others for resources or opportunities. This often leads to feelings of jealousy, insecurity, and fear.

How to Rewire:

Shift your perspective from scarcity to abundance by understanding that there is more than enough for everyone. Wealth is not a pie that gets smaller as more people take their share; it's an infinite, ever-expanding resource. Affirm, "There is plenty of money for everyone, and I am aligned with the flow of abundance." Focus on the opportunities around you, and trust that the universe is always providing for you.

6. "Money Won't Make Me Happy"

While it's true that money is not the sole source of happiness, believing that it will never make you happy can prevent you from attracting it. People who hold this belief often convince themselves that they don't need or want money, but deep down, they may be sabotaging themselves from manifesting the abundance they desire.

How to Rewire:

Acknowledge that money, when used wisely, can enhance your happiness by providing security, freedom, and opportunities to live your best life. It can also enable you to give more to others and support causes you care about. To rewire this belief, say, "Money allows me to live a fulfilled and joyful life, and I welcome it with open arms." Focus on how financial abundance can support your personal growth and well-being.

7. "I Have to Struggle to Achieve Financial Success"

Believing that struggle is necessary for success can create resistance to attracting wealth. If you believe that financial success must come with hardship, you might find yourself unconsciously resisting opportunities that come easily or flow with ease.

How to Rewire:

Recognize that success does not have to come through struggle. It's possible to create wealth while enjoying the process and maintaining a sense of peace and flow. Shift to the belief that success comes with ease, joy, and alignment. Affirm, "I am successful, and I create wealth effortlessly." Start taking inspired actions that feel good rather than forced, and trust that the universe will support you.

Rewiring your money beliefs is an essential step in manifesting financial abundance. The more you work on shifting your mindset from scarcity to abundance, from struggle to ease, the more you will align with the energy of prosperity. By recognizing and changing these limiting beliefs, you can create a mindset that supports your financial goals and welcomes wealth with open arms.

Remember, rewiring your beliefs takes time and practice. Be patient with yourself, and celebrate the progress you make. The more you affirm your worth and align with the flow of abundance, the more money will naturally flow into your life.

Abundance Rituals: Anchoring Wealth Into Your Daily Life

Abundance isn't just something we think about—it's something we embody. One of the most powerful ways to stay in alignment with the energy of prosperity is to intentionally weave abundance rituals into your daily or weekly routine.

Rituals are symbolic acts that train the subconscious mind to focus on a desired state. They're not about superstition; they're about consistency, mindset, and energy alignment. When you create rituals around abundance, you're telling your mind—and the universe—that you are ready, willing, and worthy of receiving wealth in all forms.

Below are powerful yet simple abundance rituals that help reinforce a prosperous mindset and keep your vibration in tune with your desires.

1. The Morning Abundance Practice

How you start your day sets the tone for everything that follows. A morning abundance ritual trains your mind to expect good things, primes your energy for receiving, and grounds you in gratitude. Here's a ritual you can try:

- **Affirm While You Rise**: Before your feet hit the floor, take a breath and silently affirm: *"I am open to the flow of abundance today. Wealth and opportunities come to me effortlessly."*

- **Gratitude Rampage**: While brushing your teeth or having your first cup of coffee, list 3–5 things you're genuinely grateful for. This tells your brain, "I have enough," which invites more to come.

- **Money Visualization (2–3 minutes)**: Visualize a specific amount of money flowing into your bank account. Imagine how it feels to receive it, how you'll use it, and what peace or joy it brings. You don't have to force detail—just focus on the emotional state it brings you.

This 5–10-minute morning ritual can dramatically shift your money mindset over time.

2. The Money Love Ritual

Most people have a tense or neutral relationship with money. But if you want money to feel welcome in your life, treat it like something you appreciate and care for.

Here's a ritual that helps build a loving, respectful relationship with your finances:

- **Clean Your Wallet or Purse**: Physically organize your money, remove old receipts, and make space. A cluttered wallet signals to your subconscious that money isn't being valued.
- **Bless Your Money**: When you pay for something—whether it's a coffee or a bill—silently bless the money as it leaves: *"There's always more where that came from. Thank you for this exchange."* This shifts you from lack to gratitude.
- **Track Income With Joy**: Create a journal or digital tracker where you log all incoming money, no matter how small. Every refund, gift, or unexpected credit is proof of abundance. Celebrate each one.

By honoring your money, you create a space where it feels safe to return and grow.

3. New Moon / Full Moon Abundance Rituals

If you enjoy aligning with natural cycles, the moon offers a beautiful rhythm for setting financial intentions. The new moon is a time for planting seeds; the full moon is for releasing blocks and celebrating growth.

New Moon Ritual: Calling in Abundance

- Clean your space.
- Light a candle and take a few deep breaths.
- Write out your financial goals for the next 30 days—be specific.

- Speak them aloud as if they've already happened.
- Close with an affirmation: *"I trust that what I desire is already on its way to me."*

Full Moon Ritual: Releasing Limiting Beliefs

- Reflect on what money beliefs no longer serve you.
- Write them down on a piece of paper.
- Safely burn the paper (or tear it up), saying: *"I release what no longer serves my abundance."*
- Celebrate the progress you've made since the last cycle.

These rituals build powerful momentum when practiced monthly.

4. Abundance Jar or Bowl

This is a playful yet effective way to train your mind to expect wealth:

- Take a glass jar or bowl and label it "Abundance."
- Each time you receive money, write down the amount and how it came (a job, gift, refund, etc.) and place it in the jar.
- Watch it fill up over the weeks.
- Revisit the slips during low-energy days to remind yourself how supported you are.

You can also add affirmations, notes of gratitude, or small charms that symbolize wealth. This becomes a physical representation of how supported and provided for you truly are.

5. Embodiment Rituals: Act "As If"

Rituals aren't just about what you do—they're about how you carry yourself.

- Dress in a way that makes you feel abundant—even if it's just one elevated piece.
- Sit, speak, and walk as someone who already feels prosperous.
- Upgrade small experiences: light a candle at dinner, use the "good" mug in the morning, and play music that makes you feel rich inside.

These small shifts signal to your subconscious: *"This is who I am now."*

Abundance rituals aren't magic tricks—they're energetic habits. When you perform them with intention and consistency, they begin to reprogram your subconscious and raise your vibration to match the energy of wealth.

Choose the rituals that feel good to you. Make them your own. What matters most is how you feel when you do them. That emotion—that alignment—is what the universe responds to.

As you integrate these rituals into your life, don't be surprised if unexpected money shows up, opportunities align, or you start making financial decisions from a place of confidence and worthiness. That's not a coincidence. That's alignment.

How to Become a Magnet for Wealth

Wealth is more than a number in your bank account—it's a state of being. Becoming a magnet for wealth starts internally. It's not about chasing money, but about embodying the version of you who naturally attracts it. When your energy, beliefs, and actions are aligned, wealth flows to you with far less effort than you've been led to believe.

Think about someone you know (or have seen) who just seems to "have it." They land the perfect job, their ideas take off, and they get opportunities that seem out of reach to others. It's not always because they work harder or are smarter—it's usually because they're tuned into a frequency of self-worth, confidence, and expectation. That energy draws in people, resources, and wealth like a magnet.

So, how do you become that kind of person? Let's explore the key elements of becoming a true wealth magnet.

1. Upgrade Your Identity

The first and most crucial step is shifting your identity. If you see yourself as someone who "struggles with money" or "isn't good with finances," that self-image will play out in your life over and over.

Wealth doesn't respond to effort alone—it responds to energy. You must become the version of you who already has the financial success you desire.

Start asking:

- "How does the wealthy version of me think?"
- "What decisions does she make?"

- "What does she say no to?"
- "How does she feel when paying bills, receiving money, or setting prices?"

Begin acting from that version of yourself now—not once you've "arrived." Wealth shows up in response to your inner shift, not the other way around.

Even small changes in how you dress, speak, or carry yourself can help you lock into that new identity. When you start showing up differently, money starts showing up differently too.

2. Align Your Beliefs With Abundance

You cannot outwork a mindset rooted in scarcity. If you subconsciously believe that money is hard to get, that you're not good enough, or that success will come at a cost—you'll constantly block your own flow.

Becoming a wealth magnet means identifying and releasing the beliefs that contradict abundance. Ask yourself:

- "What did I learn about money growing up?"
- "Do I believe there's enough for everyone, including me?"
- "Am I afraid of having too much?"

Then, begin replacing those beliefs with empowering ones:

- "I am worthy of wealth."
- "Money is a tool for good in my life."
- "There is more than enough to go around."

This isn't about fake positivity—it's about installing new mental software that supports the reality you want to experience. Repetition, emotion, and evidence (like tracking income, wins, or progress) all help lock in new beliefs.

3. Cultivate Emotional Wealth Now

Most people believe that once they have wealth, they'll feel peace, security, or joy. But manifestation flips that: you feel those emotions *first*, and then the external reflects it.

This is a hard truth to swallow, especially if money has been a pain point. But the more you can emotionally *embody* wealth now—before you see it—the faster it materializes.

Here's how:

- Practice daily gratitude for what you already have, no matter how small.
- Visualize your wealth goals as if they've already happened.
- Engage in activities that make you feel luxurious or abundant—even if it's a fancy coffee at home or using your best perfume on a regular Tuesday.
- Treat every pound, dollar, or euro as meaningful.

Feeling abundant *now* opens the energetic door to *more*.

4. Stop Chasing—Start Receiving

Wealth doesn't respond well to desperation. When you're constantly chasing money, you're often in a state of lack. This creates resistance.

Wealth magnets, on the other hand, know how to *receive*. They're open to unexpected opportunities, synchronicities, and sources of income that aren't always linear.

Being in receiving mode means:

- Trusting the timing (without trying to control every detail).
- Saying "yes" to help, gifts, collaborations, or mentorship without guilt.
- Noticing and celebrating *any* form of abundance: a compliment, a free drink, a refund, or even extra time.

The universe speaks in whispers before it delivers the big stuff. If you can't receive the small things with gratitude, you're sending the signal that you're not ready for more.

5. Take Inspired Action—Consistently

You can meditate and visualize all you want—but if you don't follow through on nudges, ideas, or opportunities, you block your own magnetism.

Being a magnet doesn't mean sitting still and waiting—it means moving in flow. Action becomes *inspired* rather than forced.

Wealthy people tend to act on ideas quickly. They trust their instincts. They don't overthink every detail before taking the first step. You don't have to know how it'll all work out—you just have to move in the direction of abundance with trust and momentum.

Ask yourself daily:

- "What's one small thing I can do today that moves me closer to wealth?"
- "What's pulling my energy right now?"
- "Is this aligned, or am I just forcing?"

Follow the pull. The more aligned your actions, the more magnetic you become.

Wealth reflects how you see yourself. It responds to your thoughts, your emotions, your self-concept, and the energy you bring into each room.

Becoming a magnet for wealth is a decision you make every day—in how you treat money, how you treat yourself, and how you show up in the world. It's not reserved for the lucky or the chosen. It's available to anyone willing to align with it, claim it, and receive it.

You are not chasing wealth. You are becoming the version of you who naturally attracts it. That's where the magic begins.

Chapter 9

Love, Relationships & Soulmates

Manifesting from Wholeness, Not Need

Let's be honest—most of us first come to manifestation because we *need* something. More money. A relationship. A job. A way out of a tight spot. That's completely normal. But here's the kicker: manifesting from *need* often keeps you stuck in a loop of not having.

Why? Because the energy of need carries lack. When you manifest from a place of "I don't have this, and I need it to be okay," you're reinforcing the very absence of what you want. The universe doesn't respond to your words—it responds to your *vibration*. And the vibration of lack can't magnetize abundance.

So, what do you do? You shift. You move from manifesting out of desperation to manifesting from *wholeness*—that place inside you that already knows you are complete, worthy, and safe, regardless of your current circumstances.

Let's break this down in real, human terms. No fluff. Just a truth you can feel and live by.

Neediness = Resistance

Think about a time you really wanted something—a message from someone, a specific amount of money, or a job offer—and you *needed* it to happen. You probably felt anxious, impatient, maybe even panicky. You checked your phone too often, second-guessed yourself, and started imagining worst-case scenarios.

That emotional frequency? That's resistance. That's gripping the outcome so tightly that there's no space for it to land. And often, the thing doesn't come—or if it does, it comes with drama or delay.

Manifesting from need puts your nervous system in a state of fear. And fear energy doesn't pull in what you want—it blocks it. You may still manifest things this way, but it'll feel exhausting. You'll be hustling energetically instead of receiving with ease.

Wholeness Is the Magnetic State

Now think of a time you were in your flow. You weren't chasing, doubting, or overthinking. You just *knew* something good was coming, even if you didn't have evidence yet. You were relaxed, even a little playful about it. Maybe you thought, "Of course, it's going to work out for me."

That's what manifesting from wholeness feels like.

Wholeness says: "I desire this, and I trust it's on its way—but I'm already okay right now."

It's not passive. It's powerful. You're not detaching from your desires—you're detaching from the belief that you need them to be enough.

Ironically, the more whole and peaceful you feel, the faster things tend to show up. Because now you're a vibrational match for ease, flow, and abundance.

You Attract What You Believe You Already Are

Manifesting from wholeness is about identity. If you see yourself as lacking—lacking love, money, beauty, or value—you'll attract situations that reinforce that narrative.

But if you begin to claim:

- "I am already whole."
- "I am already abundant."
- "I am already loveable."
- Then your outer world begins to mirror that back to you.

Start acting *as if* your desire is already yours—not in a fake-it-till-you-make-it way, but in a grounded, calm way. How would you walk, speak, and carry yourself if you already had what you wanted? Begin to embody that now.

You don't wait for the relationship to feel loved.

You don't wait for the money to feel free.

You *become* those things first—and watch how life starts aligning.

How to Shift From Lack to Wholeness

Here are a few real-world ways to make the shift:

1. Regulate Your Nervous System

Manifesting from need often comes from a dysregulated nervous system—when you're in fight, flight, or freeze. Breathwork, grounding, meditation, or even walking outside can help you calm your body and return to the present. When you feel safe in your body, you send the signal: "I'm okay." That safety is incredibly magnetic.

2. Ask Better Questions

Instead of "Why isn't it here yet?" try:

- "What part of me feels like I can't have this?"
- "What version of me already believes it's on the way?"
- This brings awareness and empowers change.

3. Meet Your Own Needs

If you're craving love, give yourself love—through touch, kind words, or nurturing self-care.

If you're desiring security, look for ways to ground yourself—create a plan, journal, or connect with supportive people.

The more you meet your needs internally, the less you project desperation onto external things. And that makes you more open to *receiving*.

You're Not Manifesting to Fix Yourself

Let's clear this up: manifestation is not about fixing what's broken. It's about expanding into what's possible.

You're not creating from a place of "not good enough." You're creating from a place of growth, curiosity, and joy. There's a huge difference.

Wholeness doesn't mean you never want anything—it means you don't *need* it to prove your worth. And when you stop needing your manifestations to complete you, they come in faster, cleaner, and more joyfully.

You were born whole. You just forgot.

The more you come home to yourself—the more you accept, love, and trust where you are right now—the more magnetic you become to everything you want.

Because manifesting isn't about forcing outcomes. It's about *remembering who you are* and allowing your external world to catch up.

Desire what you want. Claim it boldly. But never let it convince you that you're not already enough. That shift alone changes everything.

How to Become the Partner You Want

Let's be real—most people are walking around with a list of qualities they want in a partner. Kind, emotionally available, successful, funny, thoughtful, loyal, attractive. And there's nothing wrong with that—desiring connection is human. But here's a powerful question that flips the script:

Are you being the kind of partner you want to attract?

Manifestation, especially when it comes to relationships, is less about "calling them in" and more about *becoming* the energetic match to the love you desire. You don't manifest love by begging for it, wishing for it, or obsessively scrolling through dating apps. You manifest it by becoming love, living in love, and treating yourself with the same depth, warmth, and integrity you expect from someone else.

The truth is, we don't attract what we *want*. We attract what we *are*—or more accurately, what we believe we are.

Let's walk through what that really looks like in practice.

1. Heal What You're Hoping a Partner Will Fix

A lot of people look for relationships to fill a void—companionship, validation, financial security, or emotional healing. But when you're asking a partner to complete you, you're not actually attracting love—you're attracting a temporary solution to your wounds.

This doesn't mean you have to be perfect before love finds you (no one is). It means being *aware* of your inner world and tending to it yourself.

Start asking:

- "Where do I seek outside what I need to be giving myself?"
- "Am I hoping someone will make me feel enough?"
- "Would I want to date the emotional version of myself right now?"

This isn't about self-judgment—it's about self-honesty. If you want someone calm, present, and kind, become those things in your own life first. Not perfectly, but intentionally.

2. Build the Life You'd Invite Someone Into

Instead of focusing on how lonely you feel, start focusing on how full your life can be. Create a life that reflects who you are and what lights you up. That way, you're not waiting to be chosen—you're curating a world someone else would *love* to step into.

Think about:

- How do you spend your time?
- What do your friendships feel like?
- Are you nurturing your health, goals, and creativity?
- Do you create moments of joy, even when you're alone?

When you live fully, you radiate a kind of magnetic self-respect. You stop showing up to dates hoping someone will rescue you from boredom or loneliness. Instead, you bring joy, presence, and richness to the table—and that is incredibly attractive.

3. Mirror the Qualities You're Calling In

Take a look at your "ideal partner" list and get curious—how much of that list are *you* embodying?

For example, if you want someone who communicates openly, ask yourself:

- "Do I express my needs clearly?"
- "Do I listen with presence, or do I jump to conclusions?"

- "Am I emotionally available with myself and others?"

If you want loyalty, integrity, and consistency—check in on whether you're holding yourself accountable in those same areas.

This isn't about performing or pretending—it's about alignment. When you live in the frequency of the relationship you desire, you naturally attract it without needing to "try."

4. Drop the Checklist, Embrace the Energy

At some point, your relationship checklist needs to evolve from surface traits to energetic alignment.

It's less about "he's 6'2 and makes six figures," and more about:

- "How do I feel when I'm around him?"
- "Does this relationship bring out the best in both of us?"
- "Are we growing in the same direction?"

If you're only focused on the form, you might miss the *feeling*. But when you focus on how love should feel—safe, expansive, fun, grounded—you'll start aligning with people who mirror that.

That starts with giving yourself those feelings first.

5. Practice Loving Yourself the Way You Want to Be Loved

This sounds cliché, but it's true: the way you love yourself sets the tone for how others love you.

If you constantly criticize yourself, abandon your needs, or tolerate disrespect—you're subconsciously teaching the world to do the same. But when you set loving standards for how you speak to yourself, how you care for your body, and how you allow others to treat you, you become a beacon for people who meet you there.

Try this:

- Write a love letter to yourself as if it were from your dream partner.
- Speak kind words to yourself in the mirror each morning.
- Set boundaries not to push people away, but to honor your worth.

Self-love isn't a hashtag. It's a practice. And it creates the emotional blueprint for healthy, fulfilling relationships.

Becoming the partner you want isn't about perfection—it's about integrity. It's about living in alignment with the love you wish to receive.

When you become someone who treats yourself with kindness, communicates clearly, honors your truth, and lives a full life, love has no choice but to meet you there.

You stop settling. You stop searching. You *become*.

And in doing so, you call in a relationship that reflects your wholeness—not your wounds.

Techniques: Mirror Work, Self-Love Rituals, and Vibrational Alignment

When it comes to manifesting love—especially *sustained*, healthy love—practical techniques can help you bridge the gap between *knowing* you're worthy of it and *feeling* that truth in your bones. That's where tools like mirror work, self-love rituals, and vibrational alignment come in. These aren't fluffy spiritual trends. They're rooted in powerful psychology and energetic principles that help rewire your relationship with yourself—and by extension, your relationship with others.

Let's dive into how these practices actually work, and how to make them part of your daily rhythm.

Mirror Work: Facing Yourself with Love

Mirror work might sound simple—just talk to yourself in the mirror, right? But don't underestimate the power of this exercise. Most people avoid looking themselves in the eye. Why? Because it brings up *truth*. It reveals how you really feel about yourself.

Here's how to begin:

Step 1: Eye Contact

Stand in front of a mirror, preferably in a private, quiet space. Look yourself in the eyes. Just pause and breathe. Let whatever emotions come up—discomfort, self-consciousness, even tears—be there without judgment. This alone is healing.

Step 2: Speak Words of Love

Say out loud:

- "I love you."
- "You are enough exactly as you are."
- "You are safe. You are growing. You are doing your best."

Repeat affirmations that feel true—or just within reach. You don't have to lie to yourself. You're simply *offering* love, like you would to someone you care deeply for. That inner part of you—the one that still questions if they're lovable—is listening.

Step 3: Consistency Is Key

Try doing mirror work daily, even for 1–2 minutes. Over time, you'll notice the way you speak to yourself shifting. Self-doubt softens. Shame loses its grip. And you begin to embody the love you once looked for outside yourself.

Self-Love Rituals: Nurture as a Daily Practice

Self-love isn't just about bubble baths and candles (though those are great). It's about showing up for yourself in small, consistent ways that signal: that *I matter. My needs count. I deserve care.*

Here are a few powerful self-love rituals to weave into your life:

1. The "Sacred Morning" Check-In

Before you check your phone or get lost in the to-do list, pause. Ask yourself:

- "How am I feeling today?"
- "What do I need right now?"
- "What can I give myself before the world asks for anything from me?"

Then act on it. Even if it's just five minutes of silence, a stretch, a nourishing breakfast, or writing down what's on your mind.

2. Weekly "Date With Self"

Pick one day a week to do something purely for you. No multitasking, no productivity—just presence. Take yourself for coffee, journal in the park, cook your favorite meal and dance in your kitchen. Do it with intention. The goal is to experience your own company as something joyful, not something to endure.

3. Physical Self-Honoring

This can be as simple as moisturizing your skin slowly, speaking kind words while getting dressed, or placing your hand on your heart when you're feeling anxious. Your body isn't a project to fix. It's your home. Treat it with reverence.

The more you normalize loving acts toward yourself, the less you'll crave validation from others to feel whole.

Vibrational Alignment: Becoming an Energetic Match for Love

Now let's talk energy. Every thought, emotion, and belief you hold sends out a signal. According to the Law of Attraction, that signal attracts experiences that match it.

So, if you're constantly vibrating in frustration, insecurity, or lack, that's what gets mirrored back. But when you shift into emotions like peace, joy, worthiness, and trust, you start to draw in people and situations that resonate with those states.

Here's how to realign your vibration daily:

1. Start with Gratitude

Gratitude is one of the fastest ways to shift your frequency. Even if you're not where you want to be yet, find *something* to appreciate—your body, your breath, your growth. Gratitude tunes your energy to abundance, which love flows easily into.

2. Visualization with Feeling

Spend a few minutes each day visualizing the version of you who already feels deeply loved—by yourself and by a partner. Imagine how you walk, talk, move, and glow in that energy. Really *feel* it. The subconscious doesn't know the difference between imagination and reality—it just follows the dominant emotional imprint.

3. Music, Movement, and Mood

Don't underestimate the power of raising your vibe through movement. Put on music that lifts you up. Dance, stretch, or take a walk. Get out of your head and into your body. This is how you shift from stagnant energy to magnetic energy.

4. Mantras for Alignment

Try affirming:

- "I am love and I attract love with ease."
- "It's safe for me to be seen, chosen, and cherished."
- "I radiate self-worth, and the right people see it clearly."

Repeat them during mirror work, on walks, or before bed. Let them become your energetic baseline.

These techniques aren't about speeding up your manifestations. They're about *becoming* the version of you who no longer *waits* for love to prove your value.

When you combine mirror work, self-love rituals, and energetic alignment, you shift from "searching" to "receiving." You stop chasing, and you start *glowing*. And from that glow, love shows up—not as a rescue, but as a reflection.

Because the truth is: you were always the love you were looking for.

Chapter 10

When It's Not Working: Troubleshooting Your Manifestation

Common Blocks and Blind Spots: Why Your Manifestation Might Be Stuck

So, you've been doing the journaling. You've written your affirmations, visualized the life you want, maybe even shouted a few incantations in the mirror. And yet… crickets. Nothing seems to be shifting. It's easy to think, *"Maybe this just isn't for me,"* or worse, *"I'm doing it wrong."*

Before you give up, know this: getting "stuck" is a totally normal part of the manifestation process. Often, the reason your desires haven't landed yet has nothing to do with effort and everything to do with *unseen blocks*—old programming, limiting beliefs, and blind spots that are quietly steering the ship from beneath the surface.

Let's shine a light on some of the most common blocks so you can clear them and open up space for your manifestations to *finally* land.

1. You're Trying to Manifest from Lack, Not Wholeness

This is one of the most common (and sneaky) blocks. If your energy behind the desire is rooted in desperation—*"I need this or I won't be happy,"*—you're actually affirming the lack of it more than the presence.

The Universe, or life itself, responds not to your words, but to your *state*. If you're thinking, "I want love," but feeling unworthy, you're still vibrating at a frequency of *not having love*. That's what gets mirrored back.

Instead, shift the energy to:

- "I would love this in my life, but I'm already whole without it."
- "I'm excited for what's coming, but I'm also deeply grateful for where I am."

This balance—desire *without* neediness—is what creates energetic alignment.

2. You're Subconsciously Avoiding What You're Asking For

This one's hard to swallow, but sometimes you're not blocked because the Universe is testing you... you're blocked because part of you is *terrified* of getting what you want.

Sounds strange, right? But consider this:

- Want a wildly successful career? What if deep down, you fear burnout or being judged?
- Want a committed relationship? But you're scared of being vulnerable or abandoned again?

- Want more money? But carry guilt around being "too much" or leaving people behind?

These unconscious fears act like energetic speed bumps. They slow down your manifestations until you feel emotionally safe to receive them.

Try this: Journal on the *downsides* of getting what you want. Yes, you read that right. Explore what part of you might be afraid of success, visibility, love, or abundance. Bringing it into awareness is the first step to clearing it.

3. You're Attached to the "How" or "Who"

Another major block? Micromanaging the Universe. We often get so locked into *how* we think something should happen, or *who* should be involved, that we ignore better paths showing up.

For example:

- "I need this specific job at that company."
- "My manifestation isn't working because that person isn't texting me back."
- "It has to happen by the end of the month or else…"

But what if life has something *better* than what you imagined?

Attachment narrows your field. Trust widens it.

Instead, hold the vision of what you *want to feel*—freedom, connection, joy—and stay open to the form it arrives in. That's when magic happens.

4. You're Not Acting in Alignment with Your Desire

You can't affirm wealth but constantly undercharge and avoid looking at your bank account. You can't say you're ready for love and then ghost people or entertain emotionally unavailable partners.

This isn't about shame—it's about *alignment*. Ask yourself:

- "If I truly believed this manifestation was mine, what choices would I make?"
- "What boundaries would I set?"
- "How would I speak to myself? How would I show up daily?"

Your actions don't have to be perfect, but they need to *reflect* the version of you who already has what you want.

When you walk in alignment, even before your manifestation arrives, you shorten the gap between where you are and where you want to be.

5. You're Not Listening to Feedback from Life

Sometimes, the block isn't energetic—it's practical. You might be getting all the signs, nudges, and redirections, but ignoring them because they don't look like your plan.

Life is always speaking to you. Through patterns. Rejections. Delays. Gut feelings. Unexpected doors closing. It's all feedback. But we often resist it because we're attached to our version of how things *should* unfold.

Instead, ask:

- "What is life trying to teach me here?"

- "Where am I being redirected rather than rejected?"
- "Is there a lesson I'm meant to embody before this next level opens up?"

Shifting your perspective from *victim* to *student* can dissolve even the most stubborn blocks.

The good news? You don't need to "force" your way through these blocks. Just becoming aware of them begins to loosen their grip. Bring curiosity to the parts of you that feel scared, stuck, or skeptical.

These aren't flaws—they're invitations to go deeper.

When you do the inner work to align your beliefs, emotions, and actions, you'll find that manifestations start flowing in—not because you hustled harder, but because you got *clearer*.

Remember, the clearer the signal you send out, the cleaner the path for it to return.

How to Reset Your Energy Field

Let's be honest: life is full of noise. People, social media, news, old wounds, expectations—it all piles on. And whether you realize it or not, your energy field absorbs and responds to every bit of it. You might wake up feeling peaceful, then find yourself drained or scattered by lunch. That's not your imagination. That's your energetic system reacting to what's around (and within) you.

Just like we shower to clean our physical body, our *energy body* also needs regular cleansing and resetting. If you're trying to manifest a more aligned, abundant life, but you're carrying around energetic clutter—resentment, fear, self-doubt—it's like trying to tune into a radio station through heavy static.

The good news? You can clear it. Resetting your energy isn't complicated. In fact, it can be one of the most empowering, grounding practices you use to stay aligned with your intentions.

Let's look at how to identify energetic stagnation, and then explore powerful, doable ways to reset and refresh your personal field.

What Is Your Energy Field, Really?

You don't have to be deeply spiritual or "woo" to understand this—your energy field is simply the subtle layer of information, emotion, and intention you emit. It's influenced by your thoughts, beliefs, environment, the people you interact with, and even your physical habits.

You know that heavy feeling after being around someone who's always negative? Or that sudden lightness you feel when you're in nature or laughing with someone you love? That's your energy field in motion. It's sensitive, and it's powerful.

When your energy field is clear and strong, you feel centered, open, and magnetic. Things flow. Ideas land. You trust yourself more. When it's clogged or misaligned, you might feel tired, anxious, reactive, or disconnected from your desires.

Signs You Need an Energetic Reset

Here are a few indicators your energy field might need attention:

- You feel drained even after resting
- You're easily overwhelmed or irritable
- You keep attracting the same draining situations
- You feel "off" but can't pinpoint why
- You've been overthinking or self-doubting more than usual
- You're struggling to connect with your intuition or desires

If one or more of these resonates, don't panic—it just means it's time to come back to yourself.

Simple, Effective Ways to Reset Your Energy Field

1. Grounding (a.k.a. "Earthing")

The fastest way to reset your energy is to reconnect with the Earth. You are, after all, an electrical being. When you stand barefoot on grass, sand, or soil, you discharge built-up static—emotionally and physically.

Try this:

Stand barefoot on the ground for 5–10 minutes. Imagine any stress, confusion, or emotional debris flowing out of your body and into the Earth. You can visualize roots growing from your feet, anchoring you deeply.

No grass? A quick cold shower or even holding a rock or crystal can help stabilize your field.

2. Energy "Sweeping" Technique

You can use your hands to literally brush away stagnant energy.

How to do it:

Stand tall. Shake out your arms and legs. Then take both hands and sweep down your body—from your head, down your shoulders, arms, torso, and legs—as if brushing off dust. Do this with intention. Imagine yourself clearing away anything that doesn't belong.

Bonus: combine it with deep breaths—inhale calm, exhale tension.

3. Water Rituals

Water is incredibly cleansing—not just physically, but emotionally and energetically. It helps release old emotions and "reset" your inner space.

Quick reset ideas:

- Take a sea salt bath (add essential oils like lavender or eucalyptus for extra soothing)
- Let the shower run over you while repeating: "I release what's not mine to carry"
- Even washing your hands with presence and intention can help ground you.

4. Breathwork to Shift Your Frequency

Your breath is your power switch. Most of us breathe shallowly without realizing it. But conscious breathwork can change your entire vibration in minutes.

Try this mini reset:

- Inhale for 4 counts
- Hold for 4 counts
- Exhale for 6–8 counts
- Repeat for 3–5 minutes

Longer exhales activate your parasympathetic nervous system (a.k.a. your calm state), which helps align you energetically and emotionally.

5. Cord-Cutting and Emotional Detachment

If someone else's energy is clinging to you—an argument, a toxic conversation, or emotional overinvolvement—you may need to cut energetic cords.

Simple visualization:

Close your eyes. Visualize any energetic ties or cords between you and the other person or situation. With kindness, imagine gently cutting or dissolving the cords, and see their energy returning to them and yours to you.

End by saying: "I return to myself. I release what is not mine."

6. Intentional Stillness

Sometimes, your energy field just needs *space*. No input. No stimulation. Just you.

Try this:

Turn off your phone. Sit or lie down somewhere quiet. No music, no guided meditation. Just stillness. Close your eyes and *listen* to your body. Breathe. This reset allows your system to recalibrate naturally—like rebooting a computer.

The more consistently you clear your energy field, the less reactive, scattered and disconnected you feel. This isn't about perfection—it's about presence.

Think of energy resets as part of your hygiene. You wouldn't wait a month to brush your teeth, right? Your energy deserves the same regular care.

Because when your field is clear, *you* are clear. And from that clarity, manifestation becomes a natural extension—not a forced effort.

Faith vs. Desperation: The Energy That Makes or Breaks Your Manifestation

Let's talk about the subtle—but powerful—difference between *faith* and *desperation*. Because on the outside, they can look a lot alike. Both may involve vision boards, journaling, and affirmations. Both may even come from a place of sincere desire.

But underneath?

One says, "I know it's already on its way."

The other says, "If this doesn't happen soon, I don't know what I'll do."

One is rooted in calm expectation.

The other is soaked in emotional chaos.

The energy you hold behind your desires matters just as much—if not more—than the actions you take. Why? Because manifestation responds to vibration, not volume. You don't get what you "scream" for… you get what you *believe* is yours.

What Desperation Really Feels Like (and Why It Doesn't Work)

Desperation comes from lack. It's the emotional signature of "I don't have this and I need it to feel whole, safe, or worthy." You might say you're manifesting love, money, or success, but what you're actually broadcasting is fear, scarcity, and urgency.

Energetically, desperation pushes your desire *away*. It tightens your body. It clings. It checks the clock. It refreshes the inbox every hour to see if something has "shown up yet."

And here's the tricky part: it's not your fault. We live in a world that glorifies hustle and instant gratification. We've been taught that if we *want* something, we have to chase it down or worry about it constantly for it to materialize. But manifestation doesn't work that way.

When you operate from desperation, you're telling the Universe (and yourself), "I don't believe this is possible unless I force it." That frequency delays results, not because you're being punished, but because your emotional GPS is out of alignment.

Faith Is the Energy of "Inevitable"

Now contrast that with *faith*. Faith doesn't mean passively doing nothing. It means holding steady in the knowing that what you've asked for is already being woven into your reality.

Faith sounds like:

- "I don't know *how* it's coming, but I trust that it is."
- "I'm not going to obsess—I'm going to prepare."
- "I release the timeline because I know it's on divine time."

When you operate from faith, you take inspired action, not frantic motion. You stay open to signs, nudges, and redirection without spiraling. You become magnetic—not because you're *perfect*, but because you're *peaceful*.

How to Shift from Desperation to Faith

- **Pause and breathe:** When you feel yourself spiraling, interrupt the thought pattern. Take five deep breaths and come back to the present.
- **Flip the script:** Turn "I need this" into "I'm excited for this."
- **Focus on feeling good now:** Faith grows when you prove to yourself that you're okay—even *before* the thing shows up.
- **Detachment is key:** You can want it deeply and still not *need* it to be whole.

Remember: Manifestation isn't about controlling the outcome. It's about aligning your energy so well that the outcome becomes a natural extension of your inner state.

And that's the power of faith.

Chapter 10

Your Manifestation Daily Routine

Morning Rituals, Night-time Routines: Bookending Your Day with Alignment

If manifestation is a lifestyle (and it is), then how you *start* and *end* your day plays a massive role in the energy you carry—and what you attract.

Most people let their day happen *to* them. They wake up scrolling through notifications, responding to messages, rushing out the door, already reactive before they've had a moment to check in with themselves. Then at night, they crash into bed after hours of overstimulation, worry, or distraction, hoping somehow their dreams come true.

But here's the truth: your *first* and *last* thoughts each day are like energetic bookends. They set the tone for how your subconscious mind processes what's real, possible, and worth focusing on. And your subconscious is where manifestation really takes root.

You don't need a two-hour ritual or a perfectly curated Pinterest routine. What you *do* need is intention. Consistency. And a willingness to show up for yourself every day—even if only for five minutes—with clarity and care.

Let's walk through how you can build powerful, soul-nourishing morning and nighttime routines that align your vibration with your desires and help your manifestations flow more effortlessly.

Morning Rituals: Start Your Day on Purpose

How you start your morning is how you carry your energy into the world.

Instead of waking up *to* your to-do list, wake up *with* your vision in mind. This doesn't mean you need to jump out of bed in a high-vibe frenzy—it means you begin with intention, even in stillness.

Here are a few simple but powerful morning practices:

1. Hydrate and Breathe Before You Scroll

Drink a glass of water to wake up your cells. Then take five slow breaths, placing your hand on your heart. Connect with your body before connecting with the outside world.

2. Choose a Morning Mantra or Intention

Pick a phrase that anchors you. This could be something like:

- "Today, I choose alignment over hustle."
- "I am open to unexpected blessings."
- "My energy creates my reality."

Say it aloud while looking in the mirror. Feel it. This small act starts rewiring your subconscious.

3. Visualization + Gratitude Combo

Spend 3–5 minutes visualizing your day going *well*. See yourself showing up with confidence. Imagine one of your desires already manifesting. Then list 3 things you're grateful for—no matter how small.

4. Movement or Stillness (Your Choice)

You don't need a full workout. A 5-minute stretch, a walk around the block, or even a short meditation is enough to clear mental clutter and ground your energy.

Nighttime Routines: Reset and Recalibrate

Your nighttime routine is your energetic *reset* button. This is when your subconscious mind becomes most open to suggestion—especially in that dreamy, half-asleep state. It's prime time for embedding beliefs and releasing the day's energetic weight.

1. Digital Declutter

Try unplugging from screens 30–60 minutes before bed. Your nervous system needs space to wind down, and your energy field needs time to breathe.

2. Journaling for Closure and Clarity

Before bed, write down anything that's on your mind—stress, excitement, unresolved thoughts. Let it out so it doesn't swirl in your subconscious all night.

Then, write down a few things you *did well* today. It helps rewire your brain to focus on progress, not perfection.

3. Script Your Desired Reality

Scripting is a manifestation technique where you write about your life *as if* what you desire has already happened. Try this at night for 5 minutes. Example:

"I'm so grateful for the amazing opportunities that came through today. My inbox is full of aligned clients, and I feel so supported. Everything is flowing effortlessly…"

By doing this just before sleep, you plant those thoughts in your subconscious—where they'll continue to ripple through your dreams and emotions.

4. Sleep with Intention

Right before you fall asleep, whisper an affirmation or intention in your mind. You can say:

- "I trust the process."
- "My dreams are coming to life while I rest."
- "I am safe to receive."

This simple act lets you drift into sleep with alignment and ease.

Why These Routines Matter

Manifestation is not just about "wanting" something—it's about *becoming* the version of you who already has it. Morning and evening rituals help you step into that version daily.

They train your mind to focus. They signal your body to relax and receive. They give your heart space to feel joy, confidence, and gratitude before the world tries to shake it out of you.

You don't have to do everything listed here. Just pick two or three practices that feel good and build from there.

Because when your day begins and ends in alignment, you naturally start living in a state of trust and intention—and that's where the real magic happens.

Journaling Prompts, Affirmations, Visualization Scripts: Your Daily Alignment Toolkit

If your mind is the soil, your words are the seeds. And journaling, affirmations, and visualization scripts? These are the tools that help plant those seeds intentionally, water them with emotion, and clear the weeds of doubt.

The truth is, that most people *don't* spend enough time consciously directing their thoughts. They hope for better outcomes while writing mental stories that contradict those outcomes all day long.

But when you build a simple, meaningful practice around journaling, affirmations, and visualizing, you shift your identity from "wisher" to "creator."

This chapter gives you practical tools to help you align daily—tools you can actually use, not just read about and forget. Whether you're new to this or looking to deepen your routine, these will help you create mental and emotional clarity that supports manifestation from the inside out.

Journaling Prompts for Clarity and Alignment

Journaling is not about perfect grammar or writing a novel—it's about truth-telling. It's where you meet yourself on the page and sort through the noise to find the clarity beneath it.

Here are powerful prompts you can use regularly. Choose one per day or cycle through them as needed:

Vision & Alignment

- What does my ideal life look and feel like six months from now?
- If I fully trusted the Universe, what would I do today?
- What version of me already has what I want—and how can I embody them now?

Clearing Blocks

- What fears or doubts are surfacing for me lately?
- What stories am I telling myself that I'm ready to rewrite?
- Where in my life am I still trying to control instead of trust?

Gratitude & Magnetism

- What am I deeply grateful for right now?
- What blessings have shown up for me lately that I didn't expect?
- What emotions do I want to feel more of—and how can I create them today?

There's no "wrong" way to do this. Sometimes your pen will fly. Sometimes you'll just get one line out—and that's enough. The key is to make space for your inner voice to speak up.

Affirmations That Anchor Your New Identity

Affirmations are not about blind positivity—they're about consistent *repatterning*. When chosen and used correctly, they help rewire your subconscious mind, strengthen emotional alignment, and shift your identity from who you were to who you're becoming.

Here are affirmation categories, with examples you can try or tweak:

Self-Worth & Confidence

- I am enough, just as I am.
- I trust myself to handle anything that comes my way.
- My worth is not up for debate.

Abundance & Money

- I am open and available to receive unexpected wealth.
- Money flows to me in fun and easy ways.
- I am safe to have more than enough.

Love & Relationships

- I am deeply loved and respected for who I am.
- I attract healthy, aligned relationships with ease.
- I give and receive love effortlessly.

Trust & Surrender

- Everything is unfolding for my highest good.
- I let go of how and focus on how I feel.
- The Universe is always working on my behalf.

How to use affirmations effectively:

- Say them aloud, especially in the mirror (mirror work is powerful).
- Write them down repeatedly (repetition builds belief).
- Pair them with movement (e.g., while walking, stretching, or dancing).
- Infuse them with *emotion*—this is what activates the subconscious.

Affirmations work when they *feel* like a stretch but *don't* trigger full-blown resistance. If "I am a millionaire" feels fake, soften it to: "I am learning how to attract wealth easily." Work your way up.

Visualization Scripts: See It, Feel It, Call It In

Visualization is more than daydreaming—done with emotion and intention, it's a mental rehearsal for your future self. Your brain doesn't distinguish between something vividly imagined and something real. That's why athletes, speakers, and high performers use visualization daily—and you can, too.

Here's a sample visualization script to try. You can record it in your voice and play it back, or simply read it slowly in a quiet moment:

"Future You" Visualization Script

Close your eyes. Take a few deep breaths. Relax your shoulders and jaw.

Imagine waking up in a life that feels completely aligned. You feel rested, grateful, and excited for the day ahead. As you get up, notice your surroundings—where are you? What do you see, smell, hear?

Visualize yourself moving through your morning with confidence. Maybe you're sipping coffee on your balcony, getting ready for work you love, or walking hand-in-hand with someone you adore.

See yourself receiving great news: a payment hits your account, a new opportunity lands in your inbox, and someone gives you heartfelt appreciation. You smile. You feel proud, supported, and deeply at peace.

As you go through this future day, notice how people respond to your energy. You radiate calm certainty. You're living from trust, not fear.

Now, hold that feeling. Let it fill your chest. Know that this version of you *already exists*—you're simply aligning with them more and more each day.

Take one more deep breath. When you're ready, open your eyes.

Wrap-Up: Use These Tools, Don't Just Collect Them

These tools work best when used regularly and intentionally—not just when you're trying to fix something. You don't wait until you're unfit to exercise, right? Same goes here. Make journaling, affirmations, and visualizations your *daily energetic hygiene*.

Your mind is powerful. Your emotions are magnetic. Your words are tools. When you bring all three into alignment, manifestation becomes not just possible—but natural.

30-Day Manifestation Challenge: Activate Your Power and Align with Your Desires

Are you ready to kick-start your manifestation journey with powerful, intentional steps? A 30-day challenge is the perfect way to jump in, build momentum, and start seeing real shifts in your life. This challenge is designed to help you create new habits that align you with your desires, rewire your subconscious, and keep you focused on what truly matters.

Each day will include a simple yet effective action that helps you get closer to your goals. Whether you're manifesting money, love, success, or personal growth, the process remains the same: focus, trust, and alignment.

How It Works:

The key to this challenge is consistency. It's not about huge, drastic changes every day, but rather small, intentional shifts that add up to big results. Each day, you'll focus on one core practice from the principles we've covered in the book: journaling, affirmations, visualization, energy alignment, and inspired action.

Your task is to complete each daily challenge with intention. If you miss a day, don't worry! Simply pick up where you left off. The goal is to make manifestation a daily practice and to build the habit of working with the Universe instead of against it.

The 30-Day Manifestation Challenge

Day 1: Set Your Intention

Write down what you are manifesting in clear, positive terms. Focus on the feeling of having already received it. Hold that feeling in your heart and mind for the rest of the day.

Day 2: Journal Your Desires

Describe in detail what your ideal life looks like. Get specific about your dreams, goals, and the lifestyle you desire.

Day 3: Affirm Your Worth

Write and say aloud at least 10 affirmations that reflect your worth and readiness to receive your desires.

Day 4: Visualization

Spend 5-10 minutes visualizing your ideal reality. Picture yourself already living it, and feel the emotions that come with it.

Day 5: Clear Your Blocks

Write down any limiting beliefs that are holding you back, then write a new empowering belief to replace them.

Day 6: Energy Check-In

Tune into your energy. Are you feeling open to receiving, or are there signs of resistance? Take time to realign.

Day 7: Act as if

Take one small step that shows you believe your manifestation is already on its way.

Day 8: Gratitude Practice

Write down 10 things you're grateful for today. Feel into the abundance of your life.

Day 9: Revisit Your Vision

Read through your vision from Day 2. Does it still excite you? If not, rewrite it and make it even bigger!

Day 10: Align with the Universe

Spend time meditating and connecting with your higher self. Ask for guidance on what steps to take next.

Day 11: Release Control

Surrender your manifestation to the Universe. Let go of needing to control how or when it shows up.

Day 12: Inspired Action

Take an action that feels right, even if it's small. This could be as simple as reaching out to someone, signing up for a course, or trying something new.

Day 13: Mirror Work

Look in the mirror and affirm your worth and potential. Speak to yourself with love and compassion.

Day 14: Vision Board

Create a vision board (physical or digital) with images that represent your desires. Use it as a reminder of where you're headed.

Day 15: Clear Old Energy

Take some time to declutter or clean your space. Physical clutter can block the flow of abundance and energy.

Day 16: Revisit Your Intentions

Check-in with your intention from Day 1. Are there any shifts or new insights? Update your vision if needed.

Day 17: Affirmation Overload

Write out your affirmations 5-10 times in a journal. Say them aloud with conviction and belief.

Day 18: Creative Expression

Engage in a creative activity that makes you feel alive, whether it's painting, dancing, or writing. This helps raise your frequency.

Day 19: Connect with Nature

Spend time outside, reconnecting with the Earth. Breathe deeply and feel the energy around you.

Day 20: Practice Patience

Take a moment to reflect on how far you've come. Trust that everything is unfolding at the right pace.

Day 21: Visualize the Feeling

Focus on the feeling of already having what you desire. Sit with that emotion and let it fill your entire being.

Day 22: Let Go of Fear

Identify one fear that's holding you back and release it. Write down what's on the other side of that fear.

Day 23: Affirmative Action

Do something today that shows you trust your manifestation is on its way. It could be sending an email, making a phone call, or investing in yourself.

Day 24: Review Your Progress

Look back on your journey so far. What have you manifested already? Celebrate even the small wins.

Day 25: Write a Gratitude List

Make a list of all the things you've manifested so far. Give thanks for the people, opportunities, and circumstances that are supporting your journey.

Day 26: Shift Limiting Beliefs

Focus on one limiting belief you still carry and rewrite it into a new belief that supports your manifestation.

Day 27: Raise Your Vibration

Do something that brings you joy today. Whether it's watching your favorite show, spending time with loved ones, or enjoying a hobby—raise your vibe!

Day 28: Trust Your Inner Wisdom

Take time today to listen to your intuition. What is your higher self guiding you to do next?

Day 29: Be Open to Signs

Look for signs from the Universe today. Acknowledge any synchronicities or moments of guidance you receive.

Day 30: Celebrate and Reflect

Celebrate your progress and reflect on how you feel now. Are you more aligned? More trusting? Take a moment to appreciate your journey and everything you've learned.

The 30-Day Manifestation Challenge is a simple yet profound way to integrate the principles of manifestation into your daily life. The key is consistency, trust, and alignment. As you build these daily habits, you'll see more opportunities, synchronicities, and abundance flow into your life.

Remember: manifestation is not just about getting what you want—it's about becoming the person who already has it. And that process starts *now*.

Ready to dive in? Your manifestations are waiting.

Conclusion:

You Are the Creator of Your Reality

As you reach the final pages of this book, remember this: you've always had the power to manifest your dreams, even if it's something you've never fully realized before. Manifestation is not a magical mystery—it's a proven process of aligning your energy, thoughts, and actions with the desires you hold deep within your heart. Now that you've learned the tools, practices, and principles, it's up to you to use them.

It's time to step into your power.

The process of manifestation isn't a one-time event, nor is it a destination. It's an ongoing journey, one where you continually evolve, grow, and refine your energy to match the life you want to live. Every choice, every thought, every feeling, and every action you take contributes to the reality you are creating.

By applying the lessons from this book, you've shifted your mindset. You've broken free from limiting beliefs, released resistance, and learned how to align with your desires in a way that feels authentic and powerful. You've learned to trust the Universe, take inspired action, and become a magnet for the abundance that is rightfully yours.

But remember, manifestation isn't about *chasing* something—it's about *becoming* the version of yourself who naturally attracts all that you desire. As you continue this journey, embrace the process with patience, faith, and love. Know that you are always on the right path and that every step you take leads you closer to your dreams.

In this moment, you are standing at the threshold of possibility. The future you've always dreamed of is within your reach. Your manifestations are not out of your grasp—they are already on their way to you, as long as you remain aligned with them.

The Universe is always supporting you. You are never alone. And now, with the tools you've acquired, you can create a life that is not just *good*—but extraordinary.

Thank you for allowing me to guide you through this process. Keep your vision alive, stay in alignment, and remember that you are worthy of all that you desire. The world is waiting for your unique energy, your gifts, and your brilliance.

Now go forth, trust in the process, and allow the magic of manifestation to flow into your life. Your journey has just begun.

You are the creator of your reality.

Incantation Creation Worksheet

Use this worksheet to create powerful, personalized incantations you can repeat daily to rewire your subconscious and align with your desired reality.

STEP 1: Identify the Old Belief You're Releasing

What thought or pattern keeps showing up and holding you back?

Write it here:

_____

_____

_____

_____

_____

STEP 2: Flip the Script

What's the empowering truth you are choosing instead?

Think in terms of who you are becoming, not who you've been.

Write 1–3 bold, positive statements:

- I am _____

  _____

- I attract _____

  _____

- I choose _____

  _____

STEP 3: Activate the Energy

☐ Add physicality:

☐ Say it out loud

☐ Stand tall or move your body

☐ Add breath, rhythm, or gesture

☐ Look in the mirror and make eye contact

🗣 Try saying it with intensity, like this:

"I AM powerful. I AM focused. I CREATE results!"

STEP 4: Daily Ritual

When will you practice your incantations?

☐ Morning

☐ Before bed

☐ During your walk

☐ Before work or a big event

☐ Midday reset

Commitment:

I will repeat my incantations _____ times per day for _____ days.

Signature: _____

Date: _____

STEP 5: Track the Shift

How do you feel after 7 days? After 21?

Have you noticed any changes in mood, confidence, or outcomes?

Reflect here weekly and notice your transformation.

References

Amen, D. G. (1998). *Change your brain, change your life.* Harmony Books.

Callahan, R. J., & Chalder, T. (2001). *Tapping the healer within: Using Thought Field Therapy to instantly conquer your fears, anxieties, and emotional distress.* McGraw-Hill.

Carnegie, D. (1936). *How to win friends and influence people.* Simon & Schuster.

Chopra, D. (1994). *The seven spiritual laws of success: A practical guide to the fulfillment of your dreams.* Amber-Allen Publishing.

Csikszentmihalyi, M. (1990). *Flow: The psychology of optimal experience.* Harper & Row.

Dispenza, J. (2012). *Breaking the habit of being yourself: How to lose your mind and create a new one.* Hay House.

Dweck, C. S. (2006). *Mindset: The new psychology of success.* Ballantine Books.

Emoto, M. (2004). *The hidden messages in water.* Atria Books.

Frederickson, B. L. (2009). *Positivity: Top-notch research reveals the 3-to-1 ratio that will change your life.* Crown Archetype.

Gawain, S. (1978). *Creative visualization: Use the power of your imagination to create what you want in your life.* New World Library.

Goleman, D. (1995). *Emotional intelligence: Why it can matter more than IQ.* Bantam Books.

Hicks, E., & Hicks, J. (2004). *Ask and it is given: Learning to manifest your desires.* Hay House.

Hill, N. (1937). *Think and grow rich.* The Ralston Society.

Lipton, B. H. (2005). *The biology of belief: Unleashing the power of consciousness, matter & miracles.* Hay House.

Pennebaker, J. W. (1997). *Opening up: The healing power of expressing emotions.* Guilford Press.

Proctor, B. (1984). *You were born rich.* Life Success Productions.

Robbins, T. (1991). *Awaken the giant within: How to take immediate control of your mental, emotional, physical, and financial destiny!* Free Press.

Sincero, J. (2017). *You are a badass at making money: Master the mindset of wealth.* Viking.

Tolle, E. (1999). *The power of now: A guide to spiritual enlightenment.* New World Library.

Vitale, J. (2005). *The attractor factor: 5 easy steps for creating wealth (or anything else) from the inside out.* Wiley.

Printed in Dunstable, United Kingdom

67004539R00100